A Bookbag of the Bag Ladies' Best

written by

"The Bag Ladies"

Karen Simmons and Cindy Guinn

illustrated by

Cindy Guinn

I'm so glad you are, you!

Maupin House

Simmons, Karen, 1948-
     A bookbag of the bag ladies' best : ideas, resources, and hands-on activities for the
K-5 classroom / by Karen Simmons and Cindy Guinn; illustrated by Cindy Guinn.
        p. cm.
     Includes bibliographical references and index.
     ISBN 0-929895-41-X
     1. Language arts (Elementary)--United States. 2. English language--Study and teaching
(Elementary)--Activity programs--United States. 3. Language experience approach in
education--United States. I. Title: book bag of the bag ladies' best. II. Guinn, Cindy,
1959- III. Title.

LB1576 .S445 2000
372.6'044--dc21   00-032919

Maupin House publishes professional resources that improve student performance. Inquire about scheduling
quality, on-site professional training for schools and districts, author visits, or ordering resources

Maupin House
PO Box 90148
Gainesville, FL 32607
Phone: 1-800-524-0634
Fax: 352-373-5546
www.maupinhouse.com

DEDICATION

This book is dedicated to the first two honorary Bag Ladies, Debbie Scott and Martha Hudson, two fellow teachers and friends who have traveled the miles with us (not always comfortably), through sun, wind, and hurricanes, printing and packing disasters, car and communication breakdowns, room changes, and mood changes. Mixed with some great laughs and some fabulous meals, through it all they have ALWAYS lent their support, encouragement, help, and humor to make this book and business a reality. We thank you and dedicate this book to you.

SPECIAL THANKS TO

Our husbands, Greg Guinn and Gene Simmons, whose pride and belief in our work has helped us to follow our dreams and whose love of fishing has allowed us to travel away from them on weekends.

Rick and Melissa Forney who are always a phone call away to encourage and guide us to take those risks and "go for it."

Donna Purtell (photographer), Paula Thompson (computer graphics), Sally Pendleton and Ashley Sullivan (students and models) for adding those finishing touches.

And to all of the teachers and administrators who have attended our workshops and have encouraged us to "put it all into a book,"
this is for YOU!
Thank you

WELCOME

Dear Educator,

We are so proud to introduce you to our book <u>A Bookbag of the Bag Ladies' Best</u>. We are teachers first, and it is through the love of teaching that we started writing thematic units with hands-on activities for teachers to follow, with literature to enhance the unit and motivate students. These units allowed us to present make-n-take workshops throughout Florida and eventually other states, getting teachers excited about teaching. Having fun teaching and fun learning are our goals in this book. Here's how:

The book is divided into subject names such as history, math, etc. These subject names are just to make the bookbag fun. History really pertains to the "history of the Bag Ladies;" math actually means some tips that "add up" to great teaching ideas. What would a bookbag be without these "subjects," "homework," and "assessments"?

Next, in the introduction to each chapter you will see a replica of a Bag Ladies' thematic unit cover. These are just some of our published units, but they will help you get an idea of how we name our units. You do not need the thematic units we have previously published to understand this book. They stand alone and/or complement each other.

Being teachers has played a large part in the kind of book we have tried to write for you. We hope that you can identify with the daily routines that we laugh about as we try to juggle being good teachers and still have a family life and our own "downtime." This has led us to write a how-to book with a story line of being a teacher today, and you learn the art of making learning come even more alive in your classroom through the use of thematic units. We do all this while keeping a focus on the skills needed for testing. Do these work together? We think they do, and that they both are needed for students and teachers to maintain a love of learning and teaching.

This book has been written to make you laugh as you read and learn, so pull out a highlighter and let's be students again!

Love,

Karen & Cindy
The Bag Ladies

P.S. We wrote this book together, but like all partnerships we do some things differently in our own classrooms. We both have different strengths, and we truly believe that we work well together because we use those strengths to help each other. In our workshops we tell stories about each other and we did not want to lose that close-up view into how we work, in this book. So, you may hear stories told by one or the other of us in the chapters. Enjoy!

Project Page Format

Materials needed...

All the materials you need will be listed here. Materials are listed per student, not per class. Multiply the number listed by the number of students in your class.

Ideas for Application...

(H) History idea
(S)   Science idea
(L)   Language idea
(R) Reading idea
(M) Math idea
(W) Writing idea
 We are sure you can think of many more ways to use these ideas too!

Instructions...

Step-by-step directions on how to complete each make-n-take activity.

Blackline masters have been provided for some of the activities.

Diagrams...

When needed we have included drawings of the step to help you create the activity. Like they say, "a picture's worth a thousand words."

Table of Contents

Chapter One

How the Bag Ladies got their start.

History

How the Bag Ladies got their start.

The good news is we're teachers just like you! And we have 40 years of experience between us. We are the Bag Ladies, but we weren't always. We were just two teachers from opposite sides of Pennsylvania, 11 years apart in age, who came to teach in Florida at a brand-new school where no one knew anyone. The amazing part was we were literally thrown together by our previous principal who sent us to Orlando to learn how to "market" our school. We stayed up all night eating M & Ms and talking about how similarly we taught, even though we taught two different grade levels and that was the beginning. We've been teaching and on the road ever since, still eating those M & Ms, still brainstorming ideas, and most of all, still having fun teaching... because that's the key, isn't it? If you're going to teach something, well, doesn't it make sense that it's fun for both you and your students?

We all know that teaching every day can be a lot of hard work. Our days are never over at 3:00, our professional development spans a lifetime, and the word "burn-out," we sometimes feel, originated with teachers. How many careers have a completely new focus every few years, new objectives of the job just as you've learned the old ones, a budget that allows for few to no supplies, and the smallest amount of pay for the toughest job? So, we settled for fun and making a difference as our operative objectives. How we did this will be set up in this "bookbag" by subjects. So, ask yourself, do I want to have fun teaching while I cover all the material I have been asked to cover, and can I buy into an idea that supplements my curriculum to make that learning fun? We just say it makes the learning fun for the student, which it does, but really we would die of boredom if we didn't add the "Bag Lady" touches to our lesson plans.

When we first came to our county, the curriculum was given to you word for word. It was UNIFIED! Unfortunately, kids weren't. The second wave was WHOLE LANGUAGE, which meant to the outside world, throw everything out and teach children to read without phonics or reading books. Quite an undertaking! We teachers knew, of course, that this was not what whole language was, rather it's a way to combine all areas of teaching reading and allowing students to practice this with exposure to an abundance of good LITERATURE. This is where the Bag Ladies really got started. As teachers looked for information to teach their grade level objectives, they needed hands-on activities to add to their curriculum, good literature to motivate that activity, and an enthusiastic approach to the teaching of the theme. The Bag Ladies chose a theme, found great literature, planned super activities, and got students motivated to WANT to learn the information. Teachers, notorious for their borrowing powers came to our room and borrowed a unit, which we threw in a bag, then asked us to put together another...and another...and we were a business.

One thematic unit grew to twelve thematic units and more. We decided to invite teachers from all over our district to come to a "Bag Ladies" workshop. We think they just came out of complete curiosity to see some "real" bag ladies. To our surprise, they too were looking for units to motivate and excite both their students and themselves, and they loved the fact that they made these ideas right there in the workshop to take home and use the next day with their students. These workshops extended to schools in our own district, then to conferences throughout Florida, and finally to this book asked for by you, our peers, of the best ideas of the Bag Ladies. We can't wait to write a unit, we can't wait to use a unit in our classroom, and most of all, we can't wait to tell you how you too can be an honorary "Bag Lady" and get excited about what is happening in your classroom.

So, that's our history. But it is YOUR future. As we take you through a wealth of ideas for any classroom and show you how thematic units must be a part of every teacher's "bookbag" of ideas!

And now, because we KNOW teachers, and we know you've been sitting long enough reading this book, it's time to create your "bookbag" of Bag Lady ideas. So, grab a paper bag, some scissors, and some survey tape (in jazzy colors) and make a bookbag to hold all of these new ideas! Mostly, HAVE FUN!!!!

Make a Bag Ladies' Backpack

Materials needed...

*One medium-size brown bag
*Survey tape (3-4 ft.)
*Scissors
*Markers
*Crayons
*Rubber stamps

Instructions....

(1) Lay out brown paper bag as pictured.

(2) Fold down top (opening of bag) to about 1 in. above the bottom flap.

(3) Open to the original position.

(4) You will cut away all of the top of the bag to the fold line except the back layer. This will create the flap of the backpack. Cut edges off so they are rounded.

Ideas for Application...

(H) Store archeological findings
(S) Collect things to recycle
(L) Store vocabulary words
(R) Hold book report props
(M) Hold math manipulatives
(W) Props for writing activities

Diagrams...

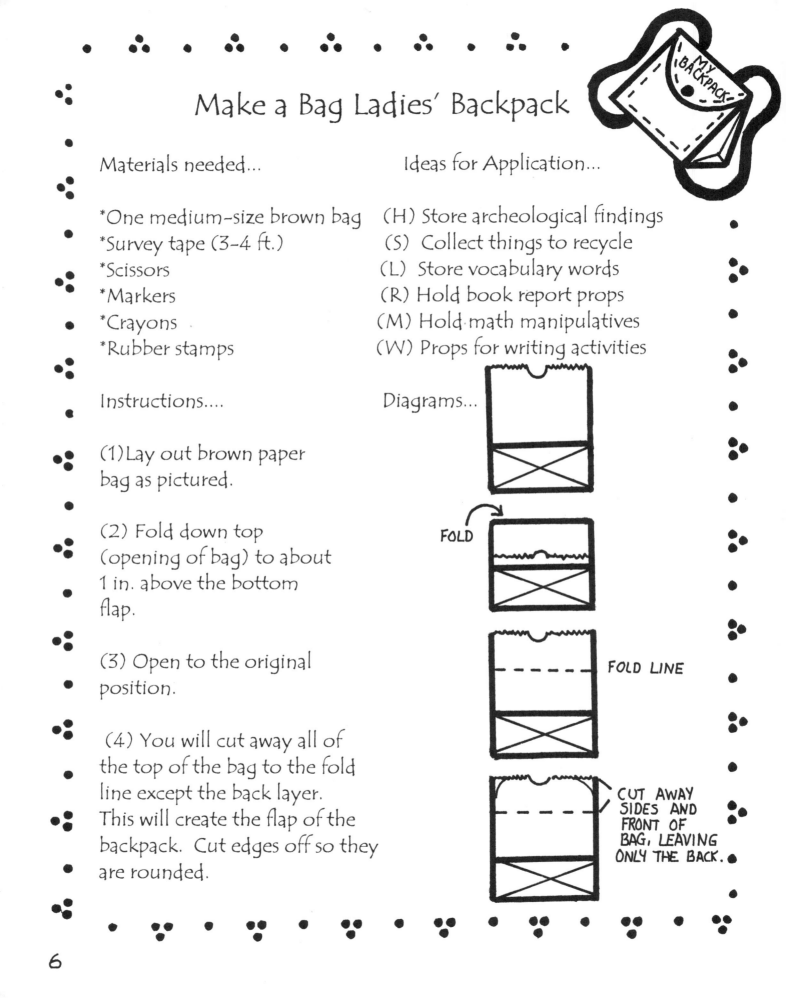

FOLD

FOLD LINE

CUT AWAY SIDES AND FRONT OF BAG, LEAVING ONLY THE BACK.

MY BACKPACK

(5) Fold flap down and flip bag over to the back side.

(6) Once the back is flipped over, draw four 1 1/2 in. lines as shown in the diagram.

(7) Open up the bag, starting at the bottom of the bag, string survey tape through the bottom slits first.

(8) Now string the survey tape through each side on the top of the bag, leaving the tape loose enough for your arms to go through the loops.

(9) Decorate backpack with crayons, markers, and rubber stamps and your backpack is ready to wear!

FRONT

BACK

Chapter Two
The typical day in the life of a teacher.
Bag Lady-style book making

Supply Box

A typical day in the life of a teacher.

Okay, so what do you need to run a fun classroom, make lots of make-n-takes with your students that still cover the curriculum you are pledged to teach, while focusing on the skills for testing in reading, writing, and math-which we like to call critical thinking skills-and have dinner on the table every night? "Too much, impossible," you say. "Not enough hours in the day," you sigh. Let's get started and organized the Bag Ladies' way!

If you're like us, your typical day does not allow time for you to plan a project and then go to find all the supplies you need for the next day. Although many of us who have taught for years think we can teach blindfolded or by the seat of our pants, trust us, it never happens, and great ideas are put on hold because of the lack of necessary supplies, organizing, and preparation of models.

Our typical day, and we are not talking about any of the extra "parent-child-husband-running-around-activities and chores" (after all, this isn't a horror story), begins by trying to get to school early enough to get morning work out on the desks (usually the math journal and problem of the day), teaching up to the last bell, leaving our classroom for umpteen meetings, etc., packing up, Did I plan for tomorrow yet? looking over tomorrow's schedule, projects, setting everything up, Oh-oh, it's pouring outside, running to pick up some groceries (I was meaning to do that all weekend), taking in dry cleaning (I'm soaked now!). You see why we left the part about picking up the kids OUT. We become frustrated and settle for not trying to get supplies for projects, supplies for great ideas, cashing a check to buy these supplies for 30. Help....the Bag Ladies are here.

Needless to say, there are many ways to be prepared. I wasn't always. Cindy is the organized one. She came in my room one day (picture this if you can), and started throwing, yes, throwing away my junk, saying, "You're never going to use this, it's buried under three boxes. You don't even know what you have!" She was trying to be nice and guess what? She was right! I knew I had pipe cleaners somewhere!

Step 1: Clean out what you already have. Put supplies you use frequently into rubber containers, label the container, and store them where you can get to them when needed.

Step 2: Write your plans for at least two weeks in advance. If they are not perfectly on schedule, you'll survive, but it will give you an idea of what you need.

Step 3: At the beginning of the year, we give each parent a letter called "Everything you ever wanted to know about grade __." The section called "supplies" looks like the next page. Only ask for the basic materials that you know you will probably use during the year. You can ask for specifics later. This list works for us. You'll be amazed!

_____Grade Supply List

Must-have's

_____ colored pencils _____ markers(thin and thick) _____ 8 regular pencils

_____ notebook paper _____ crayons _____ scissors _____ glue _____ dividers

_____ (5) 3 prong-2 pocket, pocket folders _____ 2 in. 3-ring binder

_____ scotch tape _____   _____   _____

Split-up's

Girls bring in: _____ quart baggies _____ letter envelopes

Boys bring in: _____ gallon baggies _____ legal-size envelopes

Optional Or Wish-List Items:

_____ 35mm film (Advantix) _____ colored survey tape roll

_____ craft foam sheets _____ CD cases _____ old greeting cards

_____ water colors

_____ donation $_____

As you can see, the list of "must-have's" lists those individual supplies that all students need. The "split-up's" are supplies that the whole class will benefit from but that we don't need a million of, and the "optional supplies" are materials that we find that some parents have access to, or are gladly willing to provide.

When those supplies come in, we allow children to keep their own markers, crayons, and colored pencils, along with their scissors, marked carefully, in their desks. We collect the glue and store it in bins with handles to give out during projects. We collect the notebook paper and pencils and put them in specific locations where students have easy access. Envelopes, bags, baggies, and all optional items are stored so that WE CAN HAVE EASY ACCESSIBILITY!

You also will notice that we ask for a donation of money. From this money, we purchase T-shirts (which we silk screen for field trips and field days), agendas (which our whole school uses to teach students how to be organized), and any other items that we did not request from the supply list but might be needed for projects, such as food supplies for cooking.

Since we are talking about getting supplies together for the beginning of the year, we want to give you a neat little tip for preparing your bulletin boards. Buy and cover your boards with materials that complement your theme. The room will look sharp even before your students' first day!

Speaking of the beginning of the school year makes me remember the year that Cindy came to school ready to receive her first graders (we have taught every grade which helps us to know what you will be experiencing). Her room beamed with its typical fabulous "first-day-of-school-look," complete with thematic bulletin board materials. She was called to the principal's office where he told her that tomorrow, because of the changes in population, she would be teaching fourth grade instead of first grade! He thought she would just *love* fourth grade because she loved to do writing with her first graders. Wrong! I can still hear her calling my name through the halls of the school and calling "other names" as we quickly transformed her classroom. The good news is she loved the change, proving once again that sometimes it's just the "getting there" that is so painful. We hope to make "getting there" less painful for you!

Many times teachers at our workshop ask us how we get the money for all of the projects we do with our students since the donation money seems to pay for so many other supplies. During the year, our grade groups hold fund-raisers to earn money for teaching supplies. Taking pictures of classes is one of the fund-raisers that earns a lot of money. Other grade level fund-raisers include: kids' calendars, selling T-shirts, Mother's Day flowers, Christmas poinsettias, and selling water bottles before field day. The money collected for these activities allows you to purchase the materials needed for some of your student projects.

So, yes, in order to be an organized, thematic, hands-on kind of teacher, you have to BEG! But, there is a final suggestion to filling that "supply box" without using your own money, and that is invite the parents to view where these supplies are and what they have allowed their child to learn and do. You will then receive much more than these early donations. You will receive their gratitude for a job well done, for they now have happy, achieving, motivated children who want to go to school!

Now that you've collected your supplies, let's make a book, using one of those very supplies we talked about: envelopes. You'll need two envelopes the same size and a pair of scissors for the first project.

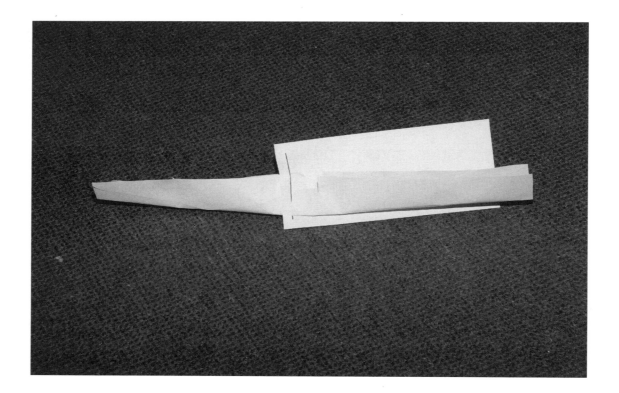

Envelope No-Glue Book

LETTERS DELIVERED BY THE JOLLY POSTMAN

Materials needed...

*Envelopes
  any size or color as
  long as they are the
  same size
*Scissors
*Crayons, markers,
  or colored pencils

Ideas for Application...

(H) Letters to the president
(S) Records of experiments
(L) Design a stamp
(R) Jolly Postman books
(M) Holds fact flashcards
(W) Letter-writing skills

Instructions...

(1) Choose one envelope to be
your cover. Seal only this
envelope.

(2) Cut off three edges of the
cover envelope, leaving one vertical
edge closed.

(3) Cut a notch in the top and bottom
of closed edge, approximately 1 in.
long.

CUT NOTCHES

Diagrams...

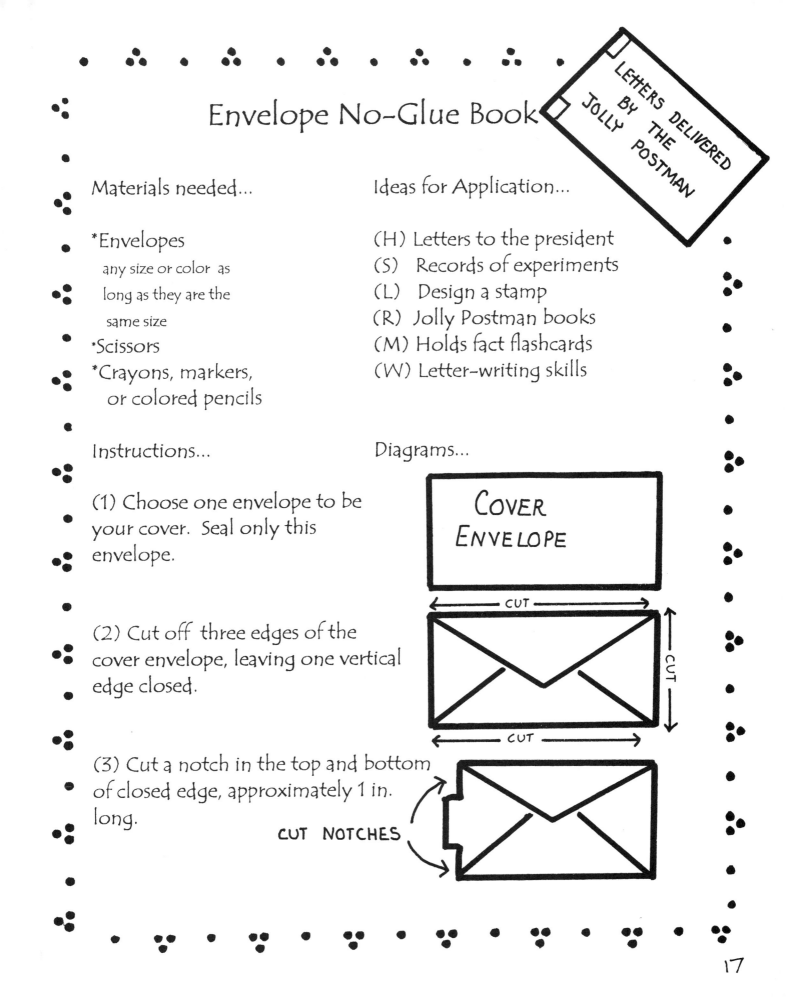

COVER ENVELOPE

CUT

CUT

CUT

(4) In remaining envelopes cut a slit along left vertical edge. Leaving a 1/2 in. space on top and bottom, and about a 3 to 4 in. slit.

SLIT →

(5) Stack all slit envelopes, matching up slits. Opening of all envelopes should be face down.

(6) Open cover envelope up and fold in half so that notches are in the middle.

(7) Slide cover through slit in stacked envelopes.

(8) Decorate cover. Address envelopes. Insert items or letters into envelopes.

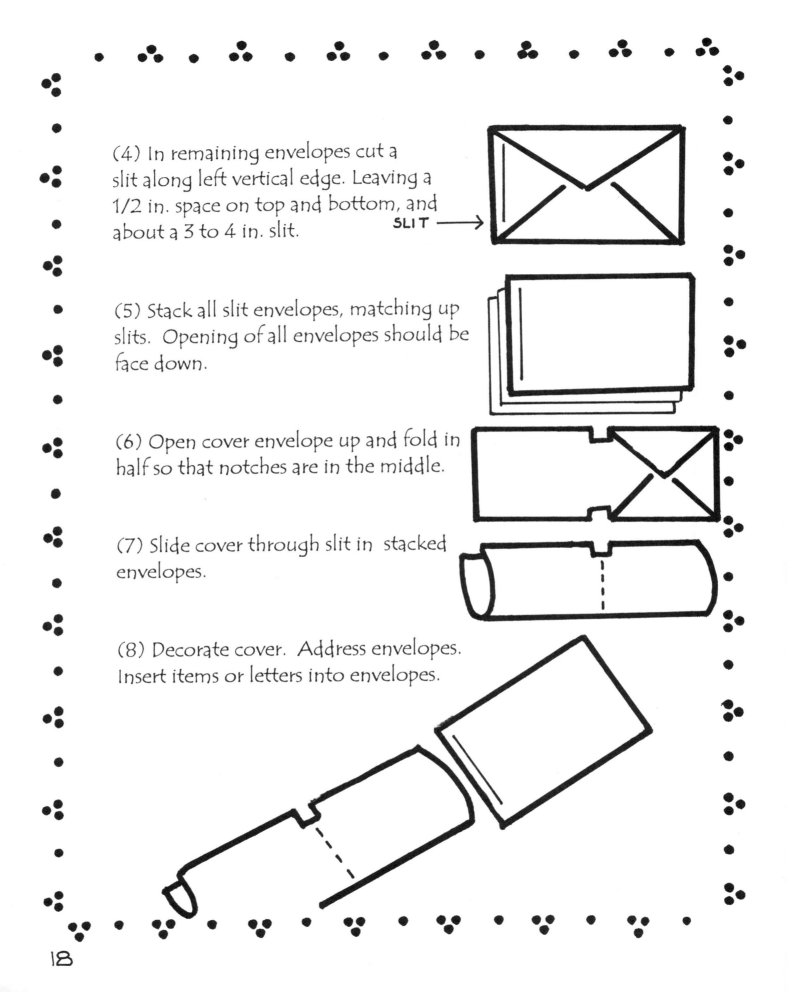

Now that you have all of your basic supplies accounted for, it's time to think about "good materials to have on hand." These might be bought with fund-raiser money or just asked for from time to time from your students, in order to build up a project materials' shelf.

*11 in. x 17 in. copy paper	This is great for making "big books" with your students. Yes, it will fit into your copy machine if it makes a book copy. Just blow off the dust from the tray because it is probably never used.
*Wide packaging tape	This is also used for bookbinding all sizes of books. Be sure to get the packaging tape dispenser too, and don't buy the cheap tape. You'll regret it later!
*Colored duct tape	You will use this to cover the outside edge of the books you make to hide the wide packaging tape.
*Black fine-tip markers	You can purchase the less expensive ones on this buy! They are great for publishing student work, and the students will think they are special.
*Paper plates	Here, the cheaper, the better is usually the rule because they have no wax on them and can be used for student coloring.

*Magnetic strip	This comes on a roll and can be found at most craft stores and teacher supply stores.
*Envelopes	You can get these free! Just stop by your local card shop after a holiday.
*Brown Paper lunch bags	Great material for all kinds of projects and, best of all, they're cheap!
*Pipe cleaners	More great project materials, and they even come in fluorescent colors now!

Some of our other suggestions: dowel rods, any size beads, white tall garbage bags, clear plastic tumbler glasses, file folders, Velcro, thin wire, brass fasteners, index cards, tongue depressors, old used or new greeting cards, buttons, sequins, glitter, and survey tape in jazzy colors (better known as crime scene tape and available at hardware stores.)

"Why?" you ask, "Would I ever need all of these supplies, and what projects will I be using them for?"

Read on and you will find a need for all of the supplies we have mentioned in your desire to be a hands-on motivational teacher.

Pop-Up or Pop-Out Books

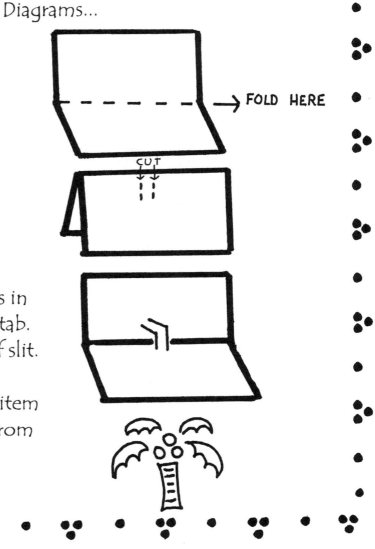

Materials needed...

*Paper-any size
*Scissors
*Glue

Ideas for Application...

(H) Johnny Appleseed story
(S) Pop out character/shadow
(L) Action pictures/verbs
(R) Pop-out characters
(M) Pop-out problems
(W) Pop-out how-to book

Instructions...

(1) Fold paper in half either vertically or horizontally. (See blackline.)

(2) With paper folded cut two slits, about 2 in. long and 2 in. apart.

(3) Open the page and push tabs in to create a fold at either end of tab. Crease at the top and bottom of slit.

(4) Repeat the process for each item to be a pop-up. Create object from construction paper to pop out.

Diagrams...

FOLD HERE

CUT

(5) Attach illustration to tab with glue.

(6) To put pages together, fold page closed so illustration cannot be seen. Glue together starting with the last page.

MY FAVORITE VACATION SPOT

GLUE

Characters Through the Page

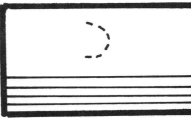

Materials needed...

- *11 in. X 17 in. white paper
- *Scissors
- *Index card
- *Crayons, markers, or colored pencils

Instructions...

(1) The class or group should decide on a character to travel through each page of the story. (See blackline.)

(2) Write a story that shows movement through different settings. Create the appropriate pictures to match.

(3) Make your character on the index card. (It helps to laminate your character.)

(4) Cut a slit in each page that is large enough for your character to travel through each page as you read the story.

Ideas for Applications...

- (H) Journey across U.S.A.
- (S) Ladybug in a garden
- (L) Describe a field trip
- (R) Character travels
- (M) Math is everywhere
- (W) Writing sequence

Diagrams...

ON OUR VACATION WE WENT MANY PLACES.

CUT OUT

GRAND CANYON

OUR FIRST STOP ON OUR TRIP WAS THE GRAND CANYON.

See-Through Books

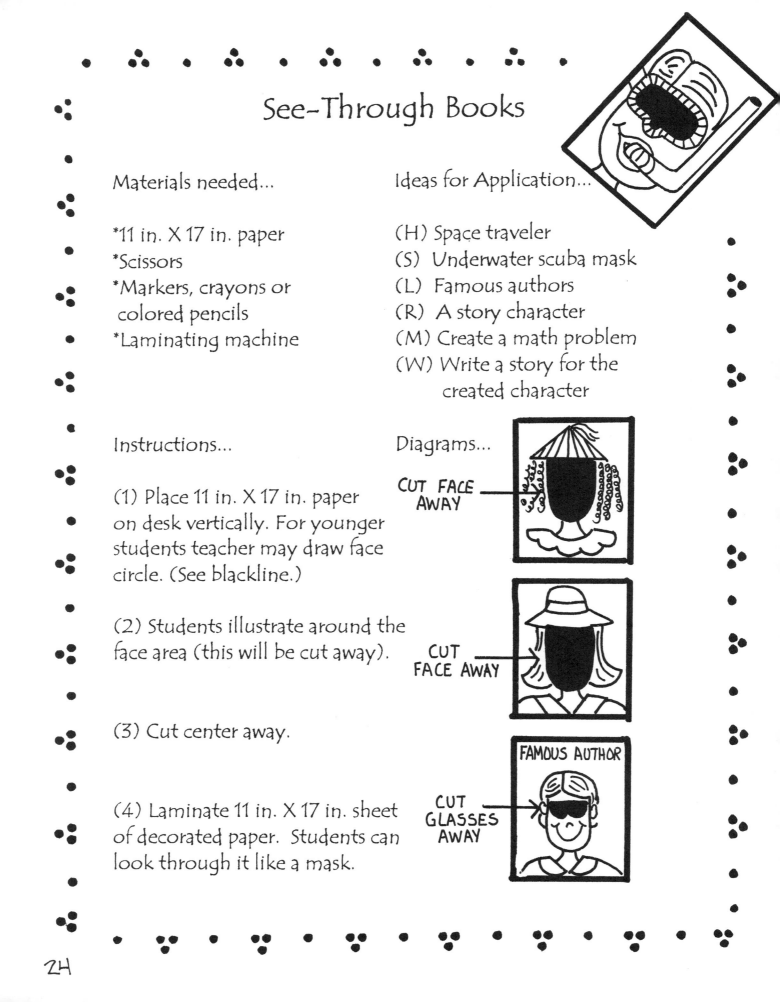

Materials needed...

*11 in. X 17 in. paper
*Scissors
*Markers, crayons or
 colored pencils
*Laminating machine

Ideas for Application...

(H) Space traveler
(S) Underwater scuba mask
(L) Famous authors
(R) A story character
(M) Create a math problem
(W) Write a story for the
 created character

Instructions...

(1) Place 11 in. X 17 in. paper
on desk vertically. For younger
students teacher may draw face
circle. (See blackline.)

(2) Students illustrate around the
face area (this will be cut away).

(3) Cut center away.

(4) Laminate 11 in. X 17 in. sheet
of decorated paper. Students can
look through it like a mask.

Diagrams...

CUT FACE AWAY

CUT FACE AWAY

FAMOUS AUTHOR

CUT GLASSES AWAY

Slide-Through Books

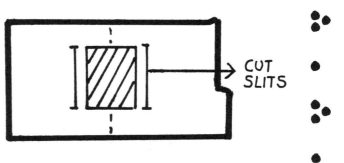

Materials needed...

*Scissors
*File folder
*Crayons, markers, or
 colored pencils
*Ruler

Ideas for Application...

(H) Map slide-through
(S) Everglades animals
(L) Vivid verbs/adjectives
(R) Sequence of a story
(M) Basic facts
(W) Picture book to prompt

Instructions...

(1) Cut a 4 in. strip off
a file folder.

(2) Cut a 4in. X 2 in.
window in the folded edge
of the open file folder.

(3) Open the folder and you
will have a 4 in. X 4 in. window
in the center of the folder. Cut
a 4 in. slit on either side of
the window, approximately
1 in. to the left and right.

Diagrams...

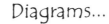

4 INCHES

4 in.

← 2 in.

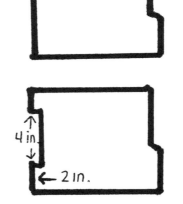

CUT
SLITS

(4) Decorate the folder with an environmental illustration, either realistic or based on fantasy.

(5) Decorate the 4 in. strip with animals to go with the environment.

(6) Slide the strip through the window and pull through to view pictures.

(7) You can write facts or story line on the back of each illustration.

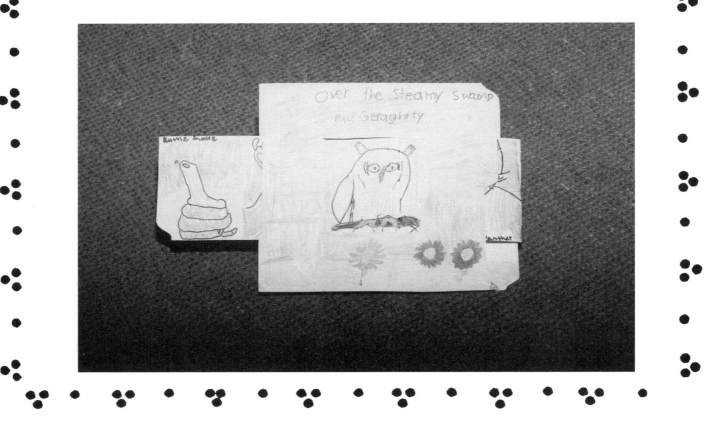

Velcro Stories

CAN YOU NAME THE STORY I GO WITH?

Materials needed...

*One sheet of 12 in. x 18 in. tagboard for background
*One 5 in. X 7 in. rectangle of tagboard for character
*One small square of Velcro per student

Instructions...

(1) On the 12 in. X 18 in. tagboard design a story setting (very colorful). Outline with black marker and color in.

(2) On the 5 in. X 7 in. tagboard create a character to go with story. Include props. Laminate characters.

(3) Place one side of Velcro square on the background and one side on the character.

(4) Students will attempt to match a character to his/her background.

Ideas for Application...

(H) Famous explorer
(S) Inventor
(L) Create story
(R) Story and character
(M) Famous math people
(W) Famous author

Diagrams...

CUT OUT CHARACTER

I'M JUDY AND THIS IS MY VOLCANO.

Character Flipbook

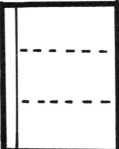

Materials needed...
*11 in. X 17 in. white paper
*Scissors
*Crayons
*Markers
*Colored pencils

Ideas for Applications...
(H) Historic people
(S) Robots of future
(L) Build a description
(R) Story character
(W) Write a story about
       a character

Instructions...
(1) Create a blackline similar
to diagram on 11 in. X 17 in.
paper. Be sure to mark the
area for placement of the
head, body, legs, and feet.
(See blackline.)

(2) Color your character
and outline with black marker.

(3) Cut on the dotted line
between the head, body, legs,
and feet. Stop at the solid
line near the binding.

(4) Teacher should bind the
pages together and share the
crazy mixed-up characters.

Diagrams...

FLIP THE PAGES
TO CHANGE
THE PICTURE.

Books for all Shapes

foods

shoe shape

holidays

animals

kite book

GREAT SHAPES FOR BOOKS

ALL KINDS OF SHAPES

geometric shapes

people

field trips

How to create a Shape Book...

Instructions...

Diagrams...

(1) Cut the cover and writing pages into the desired shape.

(2) These books bind best with brass rings and hole punches.

(3) These books work well for big books or individual small books, i.e., poem counting books (Five Little Fishes...Ten Little Seashells)

OUR FAVORITE HOLIDAY

Chapter Three
Experiment with Bag Lady style make-n-takes

How does your Garden Grow?

The BAG Ladies

Science

Experiment with Bag Lady-style make-n-takes

Whenever I see the word "science" a snapshot memory comes to my mind. Picture, if you can, I am having one of those days that we described in chapter 2, and I am so glad to be pulling into my driveway after my hectic, rainy, let's call it Monday, day. As I get the front door opened, carrying groceries, dry cleaning, and pet food, there stands my child tightly clutching a science board saying, "My science fair project is due tomorrow." Been there? Done that? Well, that's another whole book. For now, our "science section" refers to trying out a few new projects. Erase the science fair project from your mind and smile. This will be fun!

Teaching is like a science experiment. Just when you think you have found all of the materials you need to motivate and teach individual students a certain skill, your "hypothesis" of the outcome is wrong and you need to reteach in a completely different way. We invite you to try some of these make-n-takes with your students. But, remember, they are just ideas and the real measure of the success of their use is how you apply them to the curriculum you are using with your students. So, on with your apron and gloves and have fun with these "hands-on" activities. Add your own special ideas and notes in the margins as you brainstorm ways to use the ideas in your own class!

Magnetic Poetry

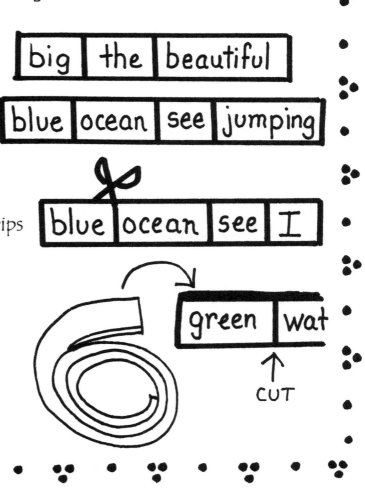

Materials needed...

*1/2 in. wide strips of white paper
*1/2 in. wide magnetic tape
*Magnetic surface to attach words: Band-Aid boxes, Altoid mint boxes
*Scissors

Instructions...

(1) Create words on 1/2 in. strips of paper and be sure to leave extra space between each word so you have room to cut. (See blacklines.)

(2) Once all words are written on 1/2 in. strips of paper, cut strips apart into approximately 6 in. lengths.

(3) Peel the paper from the sticky side of the magnetic strip and attach word strips.

Ideas for Application...

(H) Famous people and facts
(S) Plant diagrams and labels
(L) Creative poetry
(R) Vocabulary words
(M) Math facts
(W) Develop a story

Diagrams...

| big | the | beautiful |

| blue | ocean | see | jumping |

| blue | ocean | see | I |

| green | wat |

CUT

(4) Once all words are attached to the magnetic strip, cut them apart in desired places...word by word
by phrases
by sentence.

(5) Now the words are ready to be manipulated on any magnetic surface.

The big blue ocean

CUT   CUT   CUT

The   big   blue   ocean

(D) 1~2~3~4~5~4~3~2~1~2~3┐
4~5~4~3~2~1~2~3~4~5

COMPLETE THE SQUARE USING 1-2-3-4 AND 5 JUST ONCE IN EACH ROW AND COLUMN TO MAKE A SUM OF 15 ACROSS AND DOWN.

Magnetic CD Cases

MAGNETIC SPELLING PRACTICE a-b-c-d-e

Materials needed...

*Empty CD cases
*1/2 in. magnetic strip
*Magnetic sheets
* Magnetic metal
  4 3/4 in. square
*Paper
*Scissors

Ideas for Application...

(H) Historic timeline
(S) Science vocabulary words
(L) Building descriptive sentences
(R) CD case book report
(M) Review of basic facts
(W) Magnetic letters for spelling

Instructions...

(1) Carefully remove any cardboard, plastic, or tagboard from the inside of the CD case. (See blacklines.)

(2) Create a decorative cover for your magnetic CD case and slide under the tabs for the CD case front cover.

(3) Insert a piece of magnetic metal into the back of the CD case (you can find easy-to-cut metal sheets at any hardware store).

Diagrams...

THE BEST OF THE 70s

MAGNETIC VOCABULARY
boy
girl
school

INSERT METAL SHEET

(4) On a sheet of paper create a game board or just leave paper blank and insert over metal.

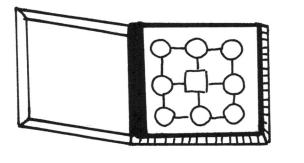

(5) Use letters, words, numbers, symbols, or pictures by attaching magnetic strip to the back. (See Magnetic Poetry for how to do this step.)

Magnetic Paint Can

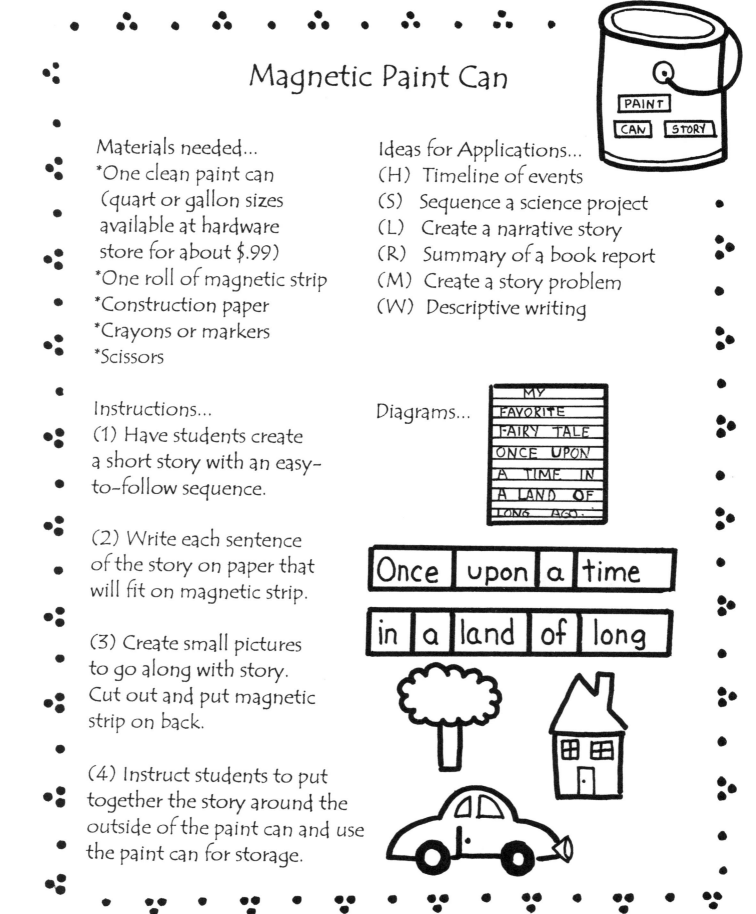

Materials needed...
*One clean paint can (quart or gallon sizes available at hardware store for about $.99)
*One roll of magnetic strip
*Construction paper
*Crayons or markers
*Scissors

Instructions...
(1) Have students create a short story with an easy-to-follow sequence.

(2) Write each sentence of the story on paper that will fit on magnetic strip.

(3) Create small pictures to go along with story. Cut out and put magnetic strip on back.

(4) Instruct students to put together the story around the outside of the paint can and use the paint can for storage.

Ideas for Applications...
(H) Timeline of events
(S) Sequence a science project
(L) Create a narrative story
(R) Summary of a book report
(M) Create a story problem
(W) Descriptive writing

Diagrams...

MY FAVORITE FAIRY TALE ONCE UPON A TIME IN A LAND OF LONG AGO.

Once | upon | a | time
in | a | land | of | long

Photograph Pose Story

Materials needed...

*36 exposure disposable camera
*8 1/2 in. X 11 in. white paper
*8 1/2 in. X 11 in. lined paper
*Glue
*Crayons, markers, or
 colored pencils
*Photo album/magnetic pages

Instructions...

(1) Take photos of students doing different actions.
EXAMPLES: Bungee jumping, driving a space ship

(2) Teacher should cut around each photo so the only remaining part is the student. The students will use this picture to create a story and illustration of them doing the action shown.

(3) Students glue the photo to their illustration and create a story to go along with it. These pictures and stories look really great displayed in a magnetic photo album.

Ideas for Application...

(H) Time travel
(S) My experiment
(L) Describe a setting
(R) Enter a story
(M) A math adventure
(W) How to...story

Diagrams...

Paper Plate Pop-Up Book

Materials needed...

*Paper plates (cheap ones)
*Paper scraps
*Glue
*Scissors
*Markers, crayons, or colored pencils

Instructions...

(1) Fold each paper plate in half separately.

(2) Cut 1 in. double slits in folded edge about 1 inch apart (2 slits=1 pop-up, 4 slits=2 pop-ups)

(3) Bend paper between the slits back and forth then push inward to create a pop-up tab.

(4) Decorate paper plate as story background and use tabs to glue items on that are to pop out.

Ideas for Application...

(H) Johnny Appleseed
(S) Life cycle of insects
(L) Descriptive words
(R) Story sequence
(M) Illustrated problem
(W) Retelling a story

Diagrams...

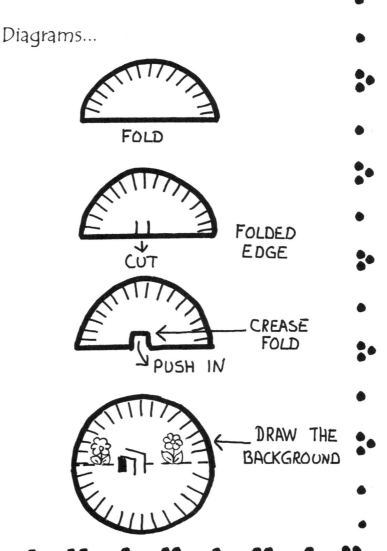

FOLD

FOLDED EDGE
CUT

CREASE FOLD
PUSH IN

DRAW THE BACKGROUND

(5) Write text around the
outside of the picture, but
inside of the ribbed edge to
create a story in the round.

(6) Close each page when
completed and put in sequenced
order. Glue back sides together.

(7) Glue half of a paper plate
to front to create your cover.
This will hide the cut tab sections.

(8) Cover the folded edge with
duct tape to give the book a look
of being bound.

Flip-Flop-Fold Book

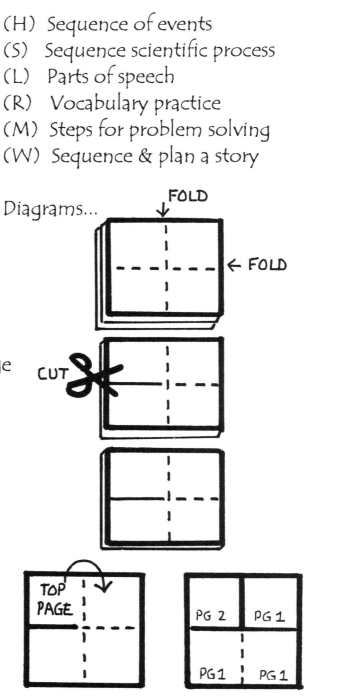

Materials needed...

*Three sheets of paper
 8 1/2 in. X 8 1/2 in.
*Scotch tape
*Scissors
*Crayons, markers,
 or colored pencils

Instructions...
(1) Stack the three sheets of
paper and fold into quarters.
(See blackline.)

(2) Cut to the center fold line
on all three pages, from one edge
to center of paper.

(3) Lay the stack of three pages
on a flat surface with the cut
edge on the left side as shown
in diagram.

(4) Fold TOP left square over
to right side of the stack.
(NOTE: You will always fold
in a clockwise direction.)

Ideas for Application...

(H) Sequence of events
(S) Sequence scientific process
(L) Parts of speech
(R) Vocabulary practice
(M) Steps for problem solving
(W) Sequence & plan a story

Diagrams...

FOLD

← FOLD

CUT

TOP PAGE

PG 2 | PG 1

PG 1 | PG 1

FLIP FLOP FOLD SOLVE THE MATH PROBLEMS FLAP

(5) Now fold two TOP squares from the top right downward continuing the clockwise movement.

(6) At the cut edge tape the bottom left square (page 1) to top left square (page 2).

(7) Once taped continue folding in a clockwise direction. (NOTE: Do not rotate the paper as you fold.)

(8) Continue the same process for the third layer, taping in the same position as the first time.

(9) Write in the text and illustrations on the 12 pages. Decorate the cover and end the book with a large illustration.

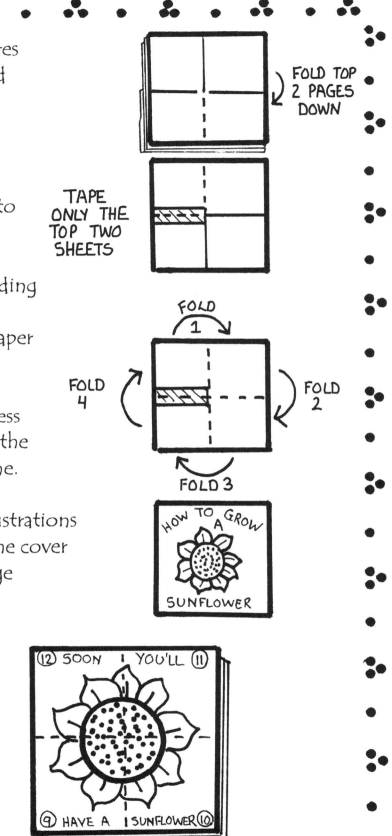

Page Protector Book

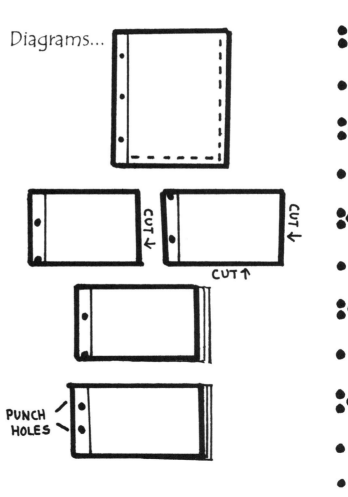

Materials needed...

*One pocket page protector
*One-9 in. X 6 in. piece of tagboard
*Two brass fasteners
*Assorted permanent markers
*Hole puncher
*Scissors

Ideas for Application...

(H) Map skills
(S) Parts of an apple
(L) Building a sentence
(R) Story scenes & characters
(M) Fractions
(W) Expository writing steps

Instructions...

(1) Cut the page protector in half horizontally.

(2) Cut apart layers of the page protector so you have four pieces.

(3) Lay all four pieces of the cut page protector on top of the tagboard.

(4) Punch two holes in the left edge of the page protector and the tagboard.

Diagrams...

CUT ↓

CUT ↓

CUT ↑

PUNCH HOLES

(5) Bind the edge with the brass fasteners, if needed secure in place by covering edge with duct tape.

(6) Begin drawing on the tagboard with a basic outline for a layered book.

(7) On each page protector add details to the base picture using permanent markers.
Example: Tagboard-State outline
        Layer 1-Major cities
        Layer 2-Major waterways
        Layer 3-State attractions
        Layer 4-State and national parks

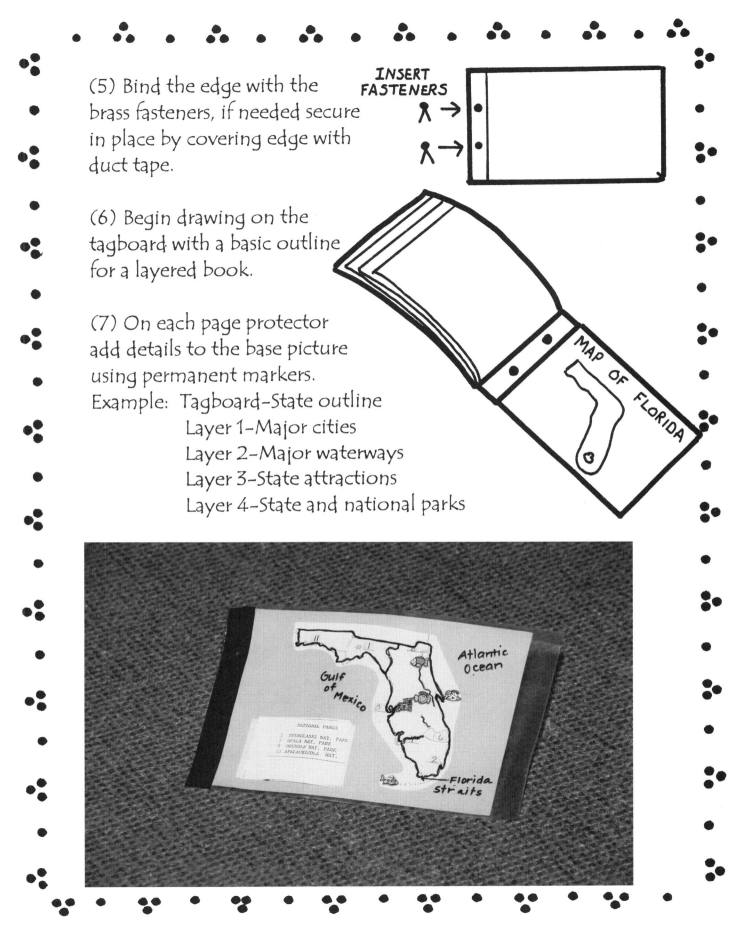

Character Slide-Through Book

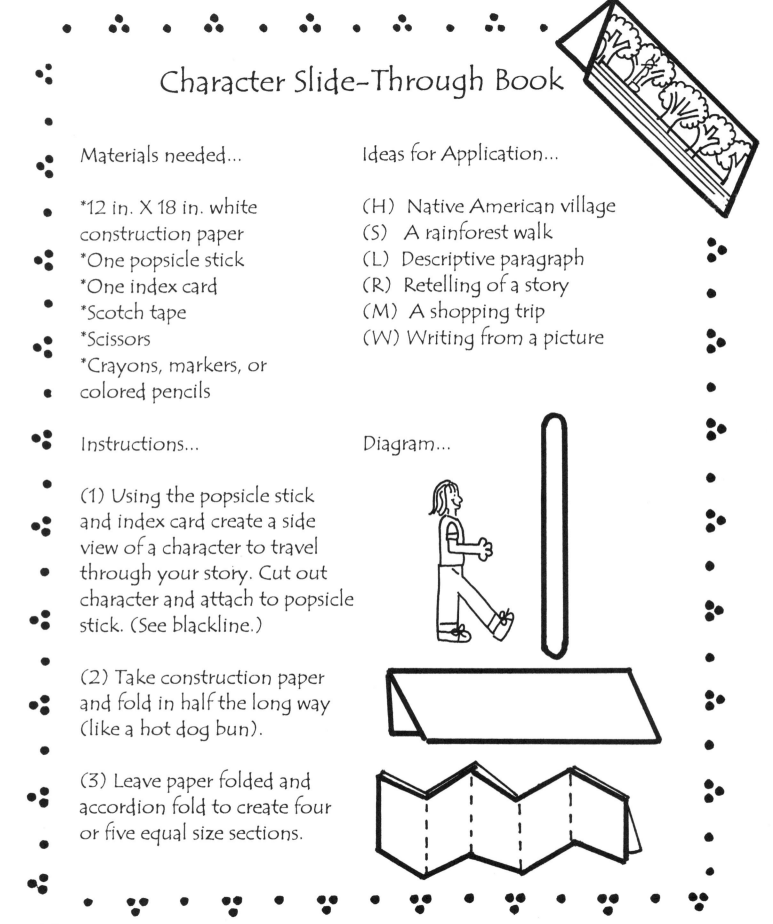

Materials needed...

*12 in. X 18 in. white
construction paper
*One popsicle stick
*One index card
*Scotch tape
*Scissors
*Crayons, markers, or
colored pencils

Ideas for Application...

(H) Native American village
(S) A rainforest walk
(L) Descriptive paragraph
(R) Retelling of a story
(M) A shopping trip
(W) Writing from a picture

Instructions...

(1) Using the popsicle stick
and index card create a side
view of a character to travel
through your story. Cut out
character and attach to popsicle
stick. (See blackline.)

(2) Take construction paper
and fold in half the long way
(like a hot dog bun).

(3) Leave paper folded and
accordion fold to create four
or five equal size sections.

Diagram...

(4) Open book after making the accordion fold to hot dog bun position.

(5) Illustrate top two thirds of the paper and write the story on the bottom third of the page.

(6) Cut a line just above your writing, one inch in from either outside edge. (Cut through only illustration side of paper)

(7) Refold the book in center and tape the ends with Scotch tape.

TAPE

TAPE

(8) Insert the stick puppet through the slit and pull through the book. To close the book, refold accordion style and illustrate the cover.

A WALK THROUGH MY NEIGHBORHOOD

Cut here

A-B-C Big Book

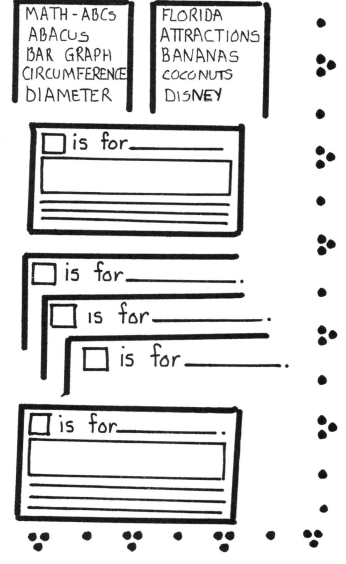

Materials needed...
*11 in. X 17 in. paper
*Construction paper
*Crayons, markers and colored pencils
*Glue
*Black fine-tip markers

Ideas for Applications...
(H) A-B-Cs of Egypt
(S)   A-B-Cs of the Arctic
(L)   A-B-Cs of verbs
(R) A-B-Cs of vocabulary
(M) A-B-Cs of math vocab
(W) A-B-Cs thesaurus

Instructions...
(1) Brainstorm words from A to Z to go with theme.

(2) Teacher or student should create a page format to be used from A-Z. (See blackline.)

(3) Once the format is decided, assign one letter to each student. Letters can than be written or stamped on each page.

(4) Each student will draw an illustration, color it, and outline using black fine-tip markers.

Diagrams...

MATH - ABCs
ABACUS
BAR GRAPH
CIRCUMFERENCE
DIAMETER

FLORIDA
ATTRACTIONS
BANANAS
COCONUTS
DISNEY

(5) Then the students will write a brief description or definition to go with each picture.

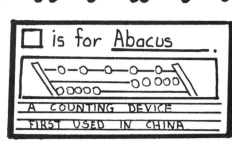

(6) Bind your A-B-C book as directed in chapter 4.

No-Glue Book

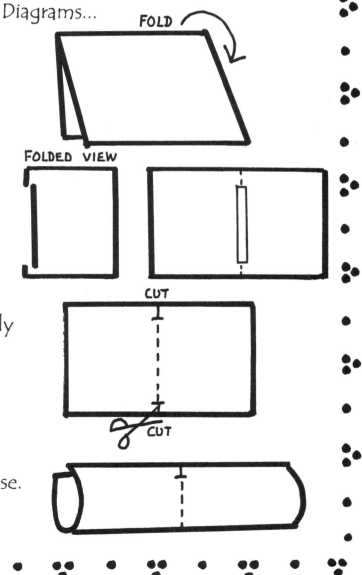

Materials needed...
*Two sheets of 8 1/2 in. X 11 in. white copy paper
*Scissors
*Crayons, markers, or colored pencils

Ideas for Application...
(H) A trip in a covered wagon
(S) My family's characteristics
(L) Write a how-to book
(R) Write a story summary
(M) Drawing graphs
(W) Publish your story

Instructions...
(1) Fold the first sheet of paper in half horizontally (hamburger fold). (See blackline.)

(2) Cut away the folded edge 1 in. in from either end of the paper (We call this a window). Set this page aside.

(3) Using the second sheet of paper. Fold in half horizontally (hamburger fold) cut a slit 1 in. in on either end of fold.

(4) Fold page with slits in half vertically (hot dog fold) so slits are in the middle but do not crease.

Diagrams...

FOLD

FOLDED VIEW

CUT

CUT

(5) Hold page with the window in the middle with the other hand so that it is opened.

(6) Insert page with the slits through the window, stopping at the slits.

(7) Unfold the paper with slits at the fold to create your finished book. You are now ready to illustrate and write your story.

NOTE: If a longer book is desired, increase the number of slit pages and insert all at the same time through the window. This is a great book for the students to make on their own at a publishing center.

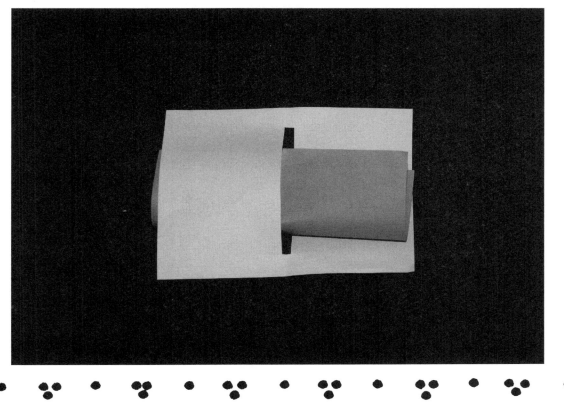

Brown Bag Book
Puppet-Style Book

Materials needed...

*Brown paper lunch bag
*Three sheets of 8 1/2 in. X 11 in. paper
*One bag puppet character
*Scissors
*Staples
*Crayons, markers, or colored pencils
*Colored duct tape

Instructions...

(1) Lay lunch bag in front of you so the opening is at the bottom and the flap is facing you.

(2) Lift the flap in the bottom of the bag and fold open end of bag in half so it lays under the flap.

(3) Open it up and insert book pages, cut pages from 8 1/2 in. X 11 in. paper, cut pages to bag size.

Ideas for Applications...

(H) Inventors
(S) 10 ways to save Earth
(L) Character & dialogue
(R) Story character
(M) Tangram character
(W) Create a story & character

Diagrams...

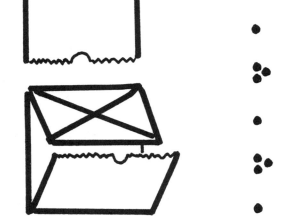

PAGES → INSIDE

(4) Staple along the folded edge to hold the pages in place.

(5) Cover the fold and staples with duct tape to create a book bound edge.

(6) Have the students create a bag puppet-style character and glue to the bottom flap of the bag as the cover of the book.

← STAPLE

FIVE LITTLE APPLES

Miami Nanny

ways to save the Earth

Step Books

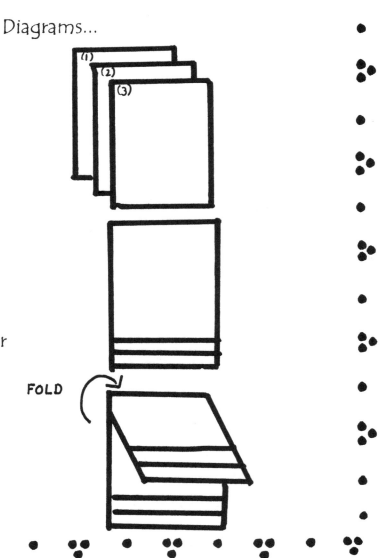

Materials needed...

*Three sheets paper
 8 1/2 in. X 11 in.
*Stapler
*Crayons, markers
or colored pencils

Instructions...

(1) Stack the three sheets
of paper so the top of each
page is 1 in. down from
the last one.(See blackline.)

(2) Flip over so varied lengths
are showing along the bottom.

(3) Fold top forward so you
see six levels of paper. Now your
book should have six pages each
being a different length.

Ideas for Application...

(H) State symbols & research
(S) Planets (use five pages)
(L) Parts of speech
(R) Fact or opinion
(M) Math facts
(W) Steps to a recipe

Diagrams...

FOLD

(4) Staple three times through all layers of paper along the folded edge.

(5) On each flap label it to go along with the theme.

(6) Now you are ready to open each flap and fill in appropriate information.

STAPLE   STAPLE

PRONOUNS
CONTRACTIONS
ADVERBS
ADJECTIVES
VERBS
NOUNS

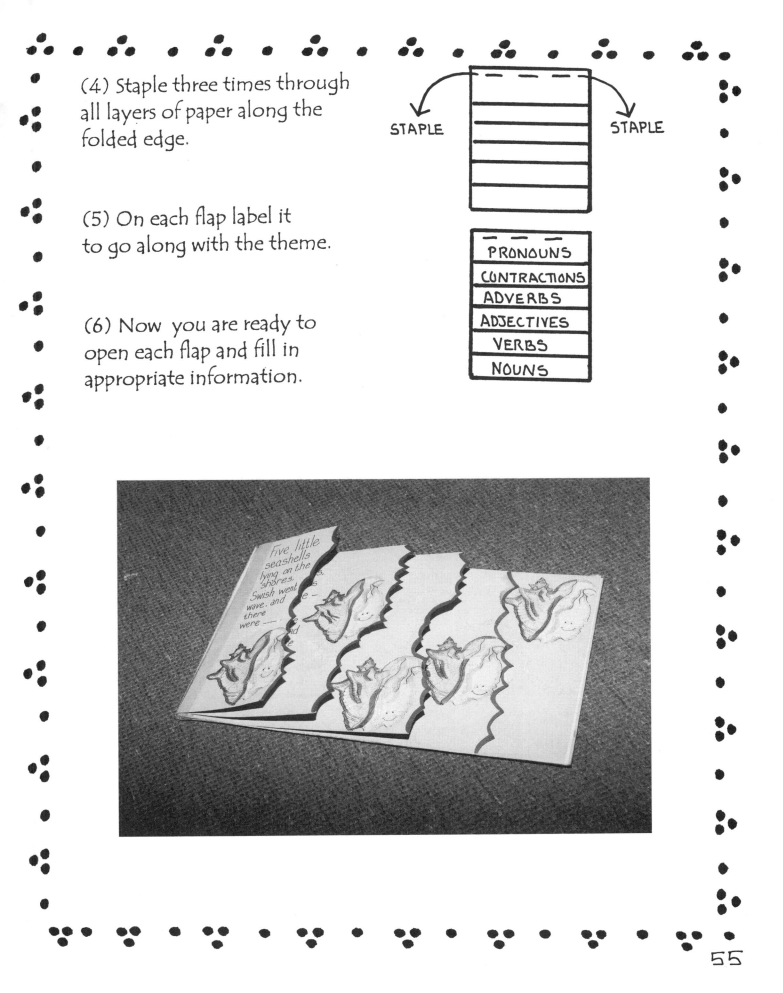

Seed Packet-Style Book

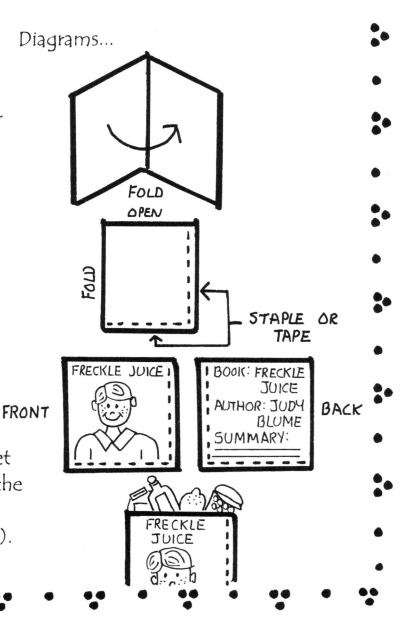

Materials needed...
*11 in. X 17 in. paper
*Construction paper
*Scissors
*Glue
*Crayons, markers,
 *Stapler or tape

Ideas for Application...
(H) Map of a country
(S) Seed packet design
(L) Rebus Story with pictures
(R) Book report with props
(M) Geometric shapes
(W) Parts of a letter

Instructions...
(1) Using the 11 in. X 17 in.
paper fold it vertically
(We call this fold a hamburger
fold. See blackline.)

(2) Staple or tape edges to
create a pocket.

(3) Illustrate front of
the pocket with topic.

(4) On back of the pocket
write all of the important
facts and information.

(5) On the inside of the pocket
make items to go along with the
theme (Seed pocket-a flower,
book report-items from story).

Diagrams...

FOLD
OPEN

FOLD

STAPLE OR TAPE

FRECKLE JUICE

BOOK: FRECKLE JUICE
AUTHOR: JUDY BLUME
SUMMARY:

FRONT

BACK

FRECKLE JUICE

Postcard Book

Materials needed...
*Paper (paper size depends on students' age), index cards work great
*Crayons, markers or colored pencils

Ideas for Applications...
(H) Postcard from past
(S) Space travel postcard
(L) Invitation writing
(R) Write to an author
(M) Send a problem to a friend
(W) Create a personal card

Instructions...

(1) First, model the correct format of writing a postcard. (See blackline.)

(2) Have the students decide on a theme for their postcards and illustrate the front. (We like to have the students watercolor the background after creating a crayon picture, a crayon resist.)

(3) On the back of the postcard students create a letter and address it properly.

(4) Students can mail their postcards or turn them into a classbook. (We like to put them into a zipper baggie book, so they can be mailed later.)

Diagrams...

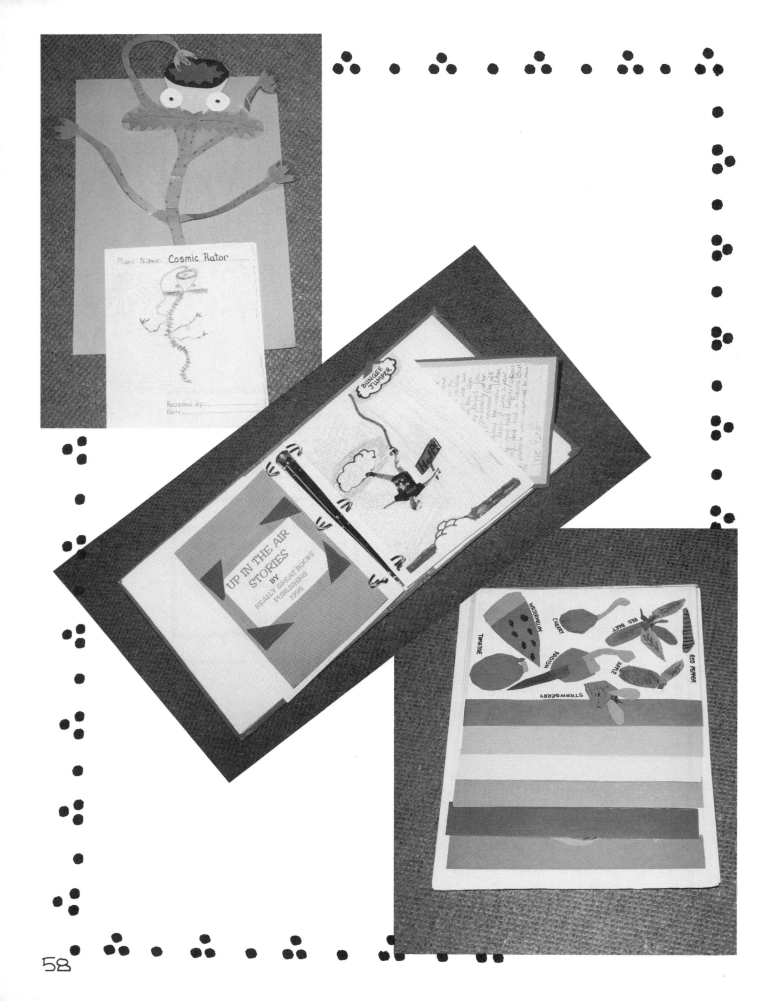

Chapter Four
The Language of getting the best from your students.
More Bag Lady make-n-takes.

Lights, Cameras, Shadows, Actions

Language

The magic of language for getting the best projects from your students.

Did you ever wish, "If I just had that magic wand, I could help this child read or that child do math problems, or help this child with his art project? (Or I could make it all disappear!)" What teacher hasn't? In this chapter we will try to give you some of our magic tricks to help you to help your students present quality projects to inspire learning.

First, whatever the project, we like to model what is expected. We used to think that this might inhibit some students from using their own creativity, but we are finding it is a successful way to introduce what we are looking for, and the student will usually build upon this model. If an art project is part of the presentation, we show our students how to draw in pencil, then, using a different media each time, students watercolor, use colored pencils, crayon, etc., and finish with "publishing markers." These markers are black fine-tip (buy cheap ones at your local office supply house) that students learn to think of as very special publishing markers. They take better care of them, and they miraculously last longer if special. Everything is outlined with these markers and it is amazing how great the pictures turn out!

Second, always display these projects in the room first and later in book form. Allow students to present to their class, other classes, and from time to time, parents. Following is a list of fun ways to make books with your students using different media, ways to bind their books, and other ways to display their projects. Students will get very involved with these activities because you are excited about them. Is it magic? You be the judge.

Multimedia Bookmaking

Whenever possible we like to vary the media used in bookmaking and in projects. By doing this, the students are excited and always looking forward to the next project. No more "I don't want to draw another picture" or "Do I have to?" or "This is boring, are we doing this again?" Your students will delight in the knowledge that they will try out different media throughout the year. Just a few ideas are the use of:

tempera paint   watercolors   pencil or ink   markers   crayon resist

chalk   pastels   collage art   finger paint   tissue paper   gel pens

colored pencils   black and white India ink   crayon   etchings   silhouettes

photographs   shadow paper   glitter glue   wet chalk

Bag Ladies hints are: Have students draw the illustration with pencil. If they are watercoloring, do that next and when dry, outline with the "publishing" black fine-tip markers.

If using crayon, outline first and then color in.

Copy artists' styles from popular children's literature. Show models to the students and watch how they duplicate the process. Some authors that this works well with are:

Eric Carle-make his tissue paper colors, but use regular white drawing paper and paint
Lois Ehlert-collage colors and step books
Bernard Most-black and white with one color
Vera B. Williams-great border illustrations

Accordion Bookbinding

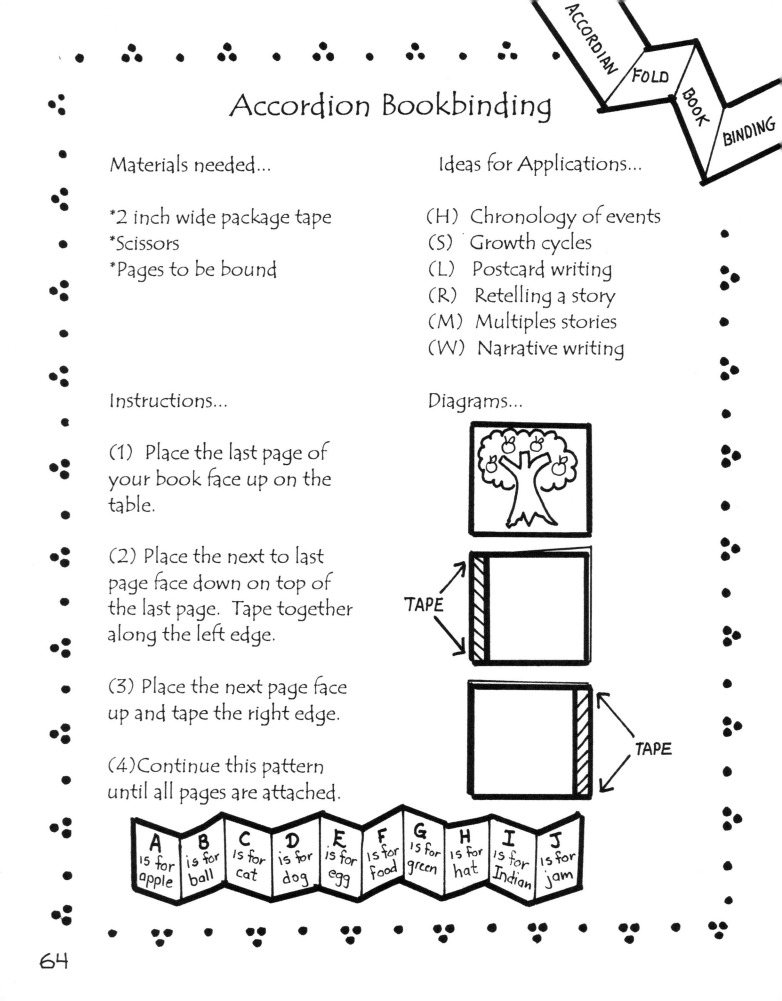

Materials needed...

*2 inch wide package tape
*Scissors
*Pages to be bound

Ideas for Applications...

(H) Chronology of events
(S) Growth cycles
(L) Postcard writing
(R) Retelling a story
(M) Multiples stories
(W) Narrative writing

Instructions...

(1) Place the last page of your book face up on the table.

(2) Place the next to last page face down on top of the last page. Tape together along the left edge.

(3) Place the next page face up and tape the right edge.

(4) Continue this pattern until all pages are attached.

Diagrams...

TAPE

TAPE

A is for apple | B is for ball | C is for cat | D is for dog | E is for egg | F is for food | G is for green | H is for hat | I is for Indian | J is for jam

Bag Lady-Style Bookbinding
including Zipper baggie book

Materials needed...

*Scissors
*High quality, extra strong
  packaging tape
*Colored duct tape
*Pages to be bound,
  including the cover
*Optional-packaging tape
  dispenser

Instructions...
Be sure to read all
directions before you
start binding.
(1) Sequence all pages to be
bound including back and
front cover.

(2) Begin binding from the
back of the book, start with
the back cover and last page.

(3) Lay back cover and last
page on a flat working surface.
Cut a piece of packaging tape
the length of the last page.

Ideas for Applications...

* Bind individual books
* Bind class books
* Zipper baggie books
* Paper lunch bags books
* Brochure book

Diagrams...

OUR FAVORITE
FIELD TRIP
BY
OUR CLASS

BACK COVER
CAN BE
TAGBOARD

LAST PAGE
Back to school.

Back to school.

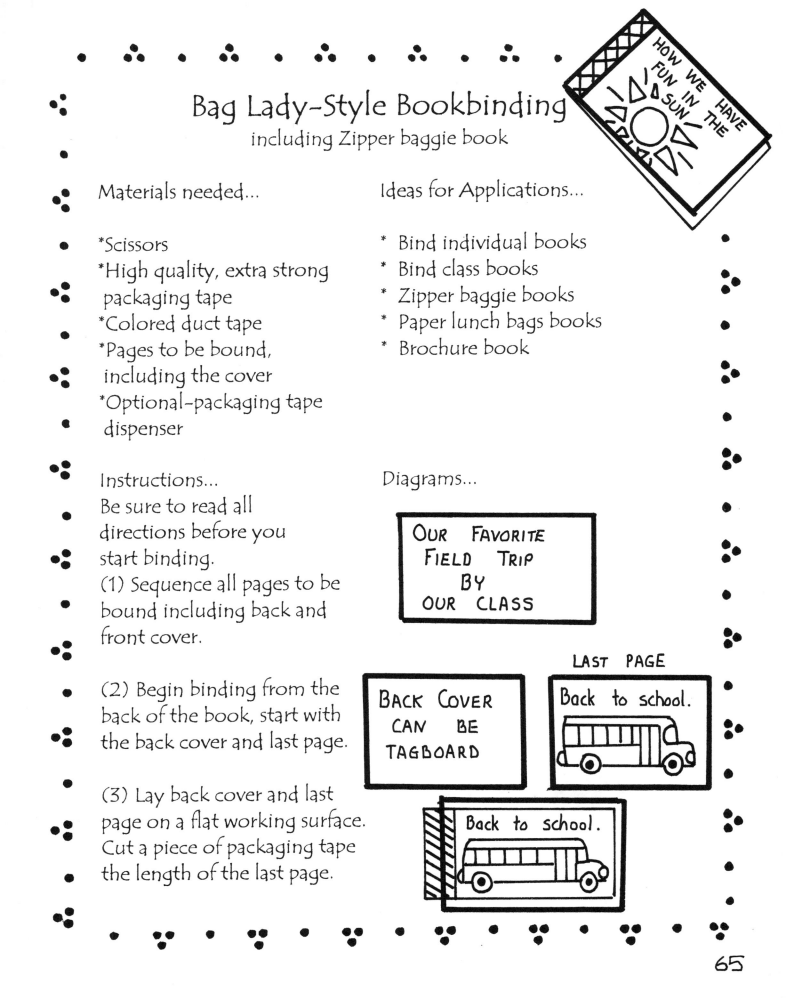

65

(4) Lay packaging tape half on and half off of the last page.

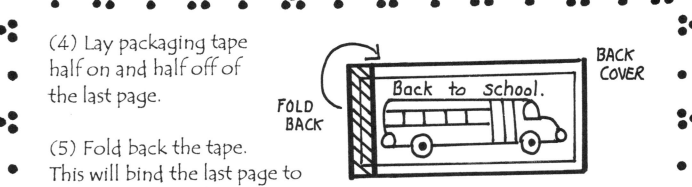

(5) Fold back the tape. This will bind the last page to the back cover.

(6) Place the next page on the top of the last page and continue taping process (steps 3-4) for each page of book. Tape ONLY one page at a time and fold the tape to back cover as each page is added.

IMPORTANT: DO NOT make the tape longer than the book pages.

(7) After taping front cover on with packaging tape, cut a piece of duct tape the length of the cover's bound edge. Place the duct tape over the packaging tape to create a bound look to the book. If the book is very thick run an additional piece of duct tape up the back side of bound edge to cover the remainder of packaging tape.

Magazine Cover Book

Materials needed...

*12 in. X 18 in. drawing paper
*Tempera paint, asst. colors
*Brushes
*Water
*Brush cleaning cups
*Black markers

Instructions...

(1) Students paint the title of the magazine across the top of the 12 in. X 18 in. paper. Paper should be vertical.

(2) They draw and paint their portrait on the same paper. When picture is dry, paint the background. Allow picture to dry and outline portrait with black marker.

(3) Students then write to the following prompt...
"I (their name)want to be known in the year 20__ as _____.

Ideas for Applications...

(H) What are you famous for?
(S) Modern science magazine
(L) Describe a person
(R) Book of the year
(M) Famous mathematicians
(W) Writing biographies

Diagrams...

MODERN SCIENCE

MODERN SCIENCE

IN THE YEAR 2020 I WANT TO BE KNOWN AS A GREAT INVENTOR.

TIMES NEWS
PERSON OF THE YEAR...

(4) Students write about what they would do, why they would do it, how and where.

(5) After editing their story students type the story on the computer and glue article to the bottom of the page.

MAGAZINE TITLE → TIMES

STUDENT PORTRAIT →

STORY →

Film Strip Projects

Materials needed...
* *8 1/2 in. X 11 in. copy paper
* *Black fine-tip markers
* *Scotch tape
* *Overhead transparencies for copy machines
* *Assorted colors of permanent markers

Ideas for Application...
* (H) Historic events
* (S) Explain scientific process
* (L) Sequence of events
* (R) Book report
* (M) Multiplication stories
* (W) How-to...stories

Instructions...

(1) See the blackline master that resembles a film strip. Make a copy for each student.

(2) Use a pencil to illustrate and write a story on the film strip blackline (DO NOT COLOR).

(3) Teacher will copy film strip with drawings on to an overhead transparency using the copy machine. Have students cut the overhead in half to create a film strip sequence.

Diagrams...

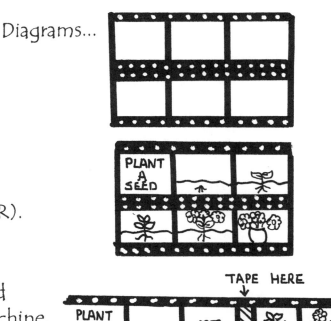

(4) Using permanent markers, students should color on the backside blackline of each panel. Please note coloring on the front side may cause black pen to smear. Students can use the film strip to give an oral presentation on the overhead projector.

Brown Bag Presentations

Materials needed...

- *Brown paper grocery bag
- *Construction paper
- *Markers
- *Crayons
- *Scissors
- *Glue

Instructions...

(1) Students each choose a topic for their bag. Draw an illustration on the front of bag. If there is printing on the page glue construction paper to cover, then draw.

(2) Ask students to research their topic and put 5-10 items in their bag to go with topic. Limit the number of pictures and photos they're allowed to use.

(3) Students use these items in the bag as props for an oral presentation, explaining why they put these items in the bag. The teacher should model this style of report first as a guide for the students.

Ideas for Applications...

(H) State report in a bag
(S) Science experiment in a bag
(L) Riddle in a bag
(R) Book report in a bag
(M) Things to measure in a bag
(W) Autobiography in a bag

Diagrams...

MAKE THE LIGHT BULB LIGHT...

PENNSYLVANIA

LIBERTY BELL

CHARCOAL FOR COAL MINES

APPLES

QUAKER STATE OIL

GRAPE VINEYARDS

HERSHEY

STEELER'S FOOTBALL

Dial-a-Story
A paper plate activity

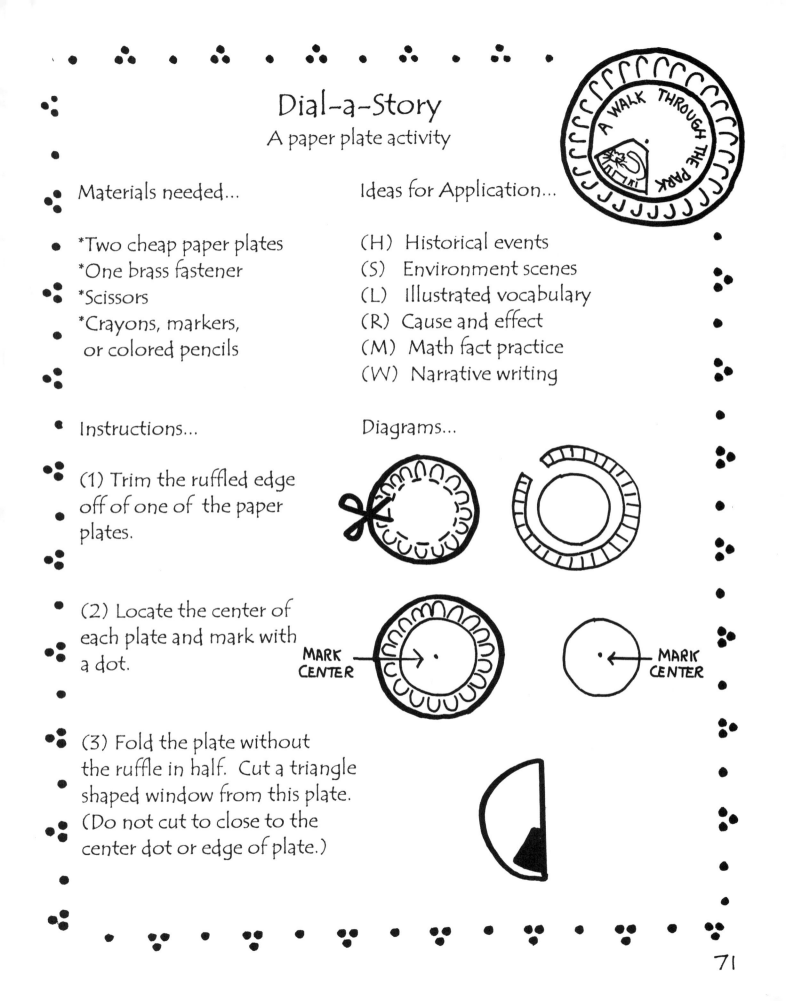

Materials needed...

*Two cheap paper plates
*One brass fastener
*Scissors
*Crayons, markers,
 or colored pencils

Ideas for Application...

(H) Historical events
(S) Environment scenes
(L) Illustrated vocabulary
(R) Cause and effect
(M) Math fact practice
(W) Narrative writing

Instructions...

(1) Trim the ruffled edge
off of one of the paper
plates.

(2) Locate the center of
each plate and mark with
a dot.

(3) Fold the plate without
the ruffle in half. Cut a triangle
shaped window from this plate.
(Do not cut to close to the
center dot or edge of plate.)

Diagrams...

MARK CENTER

MARK CENTER

(4) Open the cut paper plate and place on top of the uncut plate. Fasten together with a brass fastener.

ATTACH WITH FASTENER

(5) To decorate, students can create an illustration on the small plate and write a sequence of events in the window. Turn plate to see each event.

MAKE INNER CIRCLE LOOK LIKE EARTH

IN WINDOW SHOW ENVIRONMENTS

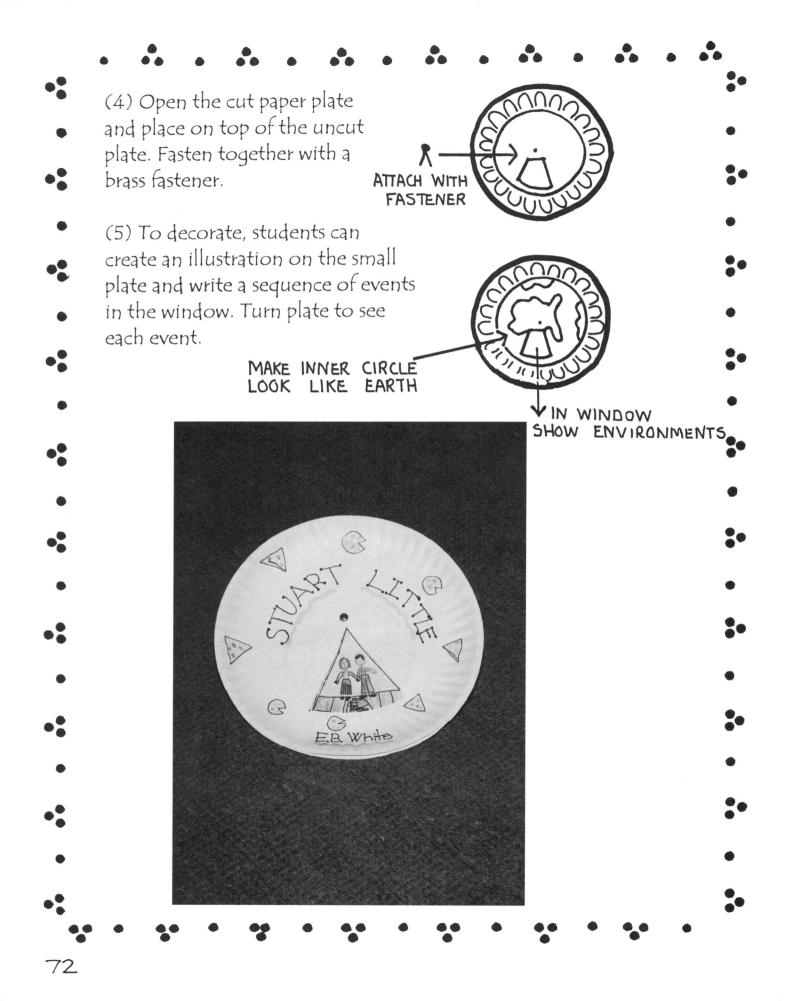

Paper Plate-arama

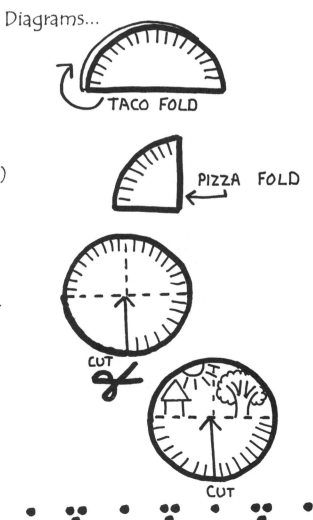

Materials needed...

*Four cheap paper plates
*Construction paper scraps
*Glue
*Scotch tape
*Stapler
*Crayons, markers, or
 colored pencils

Ideas for Application...

(H) Name a historic scene
(S) Steps to building a garden
(L) Compare story versions
(R) Re-create a story scene
(M) What do you do at _:00?
(W) Create a scene and write

Instructions...

(1) Fold each plate in half.
(We call this a taco fold.)

(2) Fold each plate in half
again. (We call this a pizza fold.)

(3) Open the folded plates and
cut one fold line to the center
of the plate. Do this on all four
paper plates.

(4) Draw a background on the
top half of each paper plate.

Diagrams...

TACO FOLD

PIZZA FOLD

CUT

CUT

(5) Overlap the two bottom pieces of the plate and tape or staple the sides together.

(6) Add stand-up characters or decorations.

(7) Tape or staple each paper plate together along the back sides. REMEMBER: Glue them together in the proper order.

SLIDE UNDER OTHER SIDE AND TAPE

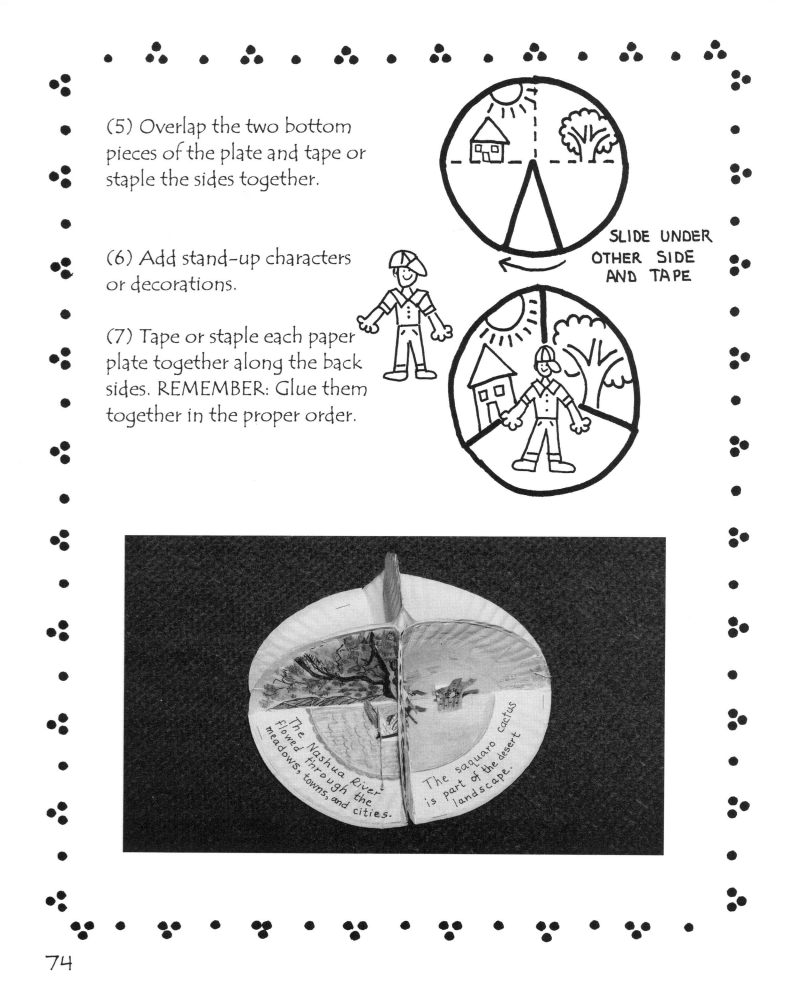

The Nashua River flowed through the meadows, towns, and cities.

The saguaro cactus is part of the desert landscape.

Story Time Capsule

Materials needed...

*Two clear plastic tumbler style glasses
*Small items for capsule
*Scraps of paper
*Scissors
*Glue
*Crayons, markers, or pencils

Instructions...

(1) Students select a topic for their time capsule as part of a cumulative review activity.

(2) Gather or create items to be placed in the time capsule. Note: Be sure to use a mixture of flat and 3-D items. Also keep the size of cups in mind.

(3) Place all items inside plastic tumbler cups and secure with packaging tape or hot glue.

Ideas for Application...

(H) Scenes from history
(S) Future time capsule
(L) Word time capsule
(R) Book report capsule
(M) Estimating capsule
(W) Create a scene & write

Diagrams...

MY BOOK IS CHARLIE & THE CHOCOLATE FACTORY.

BLUEBERRIES

GOLD TICKET

WONKA CANDY

JAW BREAKER

TV SET

Scrapbook Projects

Materials needed...
*Manilla paper or
black construction paper
*Looseleaf notebook or
self-made tagboard covers
*Glue
*Markers
*Paper scraps

Instructions...
(1) Students choose a
scrapbook cover using a
looseleaf notebook, a
purchased scrapbook, or a
student-created tagboard
cover with manilla pages.

(2) After choosing a topic
students create a scrapbook
with each page having a
theme (examples: setting,
character, plot, important
events, ending, and my
opinion).

(3) This scrapbook can be
kept as a record of a student's
progress throughout the year.

Diagrams...
(H) Famous faces from history
(S) Space scrapbook
(L) Parts of speech scrapbook
(R) Book report scrapbook
(M) Story problem scrapbook
(W) Scrapbook of my writing

Diagrams...

Bag Lady-Style Brochures

Materials needed...

*8 1/2 in. X 11 in. paper
*Crayons
*Markers
*Colored pencils

Instructions...

(1) Have the students tri-fold the paper the way a travel brochure is folded. (See blackline.)

(2) Once paper is tri-folded, have the students create a title page or cover of their brochure.

(3) It is helpful to give the students a guideline for each page, but that is optional.

Ideas for Application...

(H) Historical tourist site
(S) Science experiment
(L) What is a noun?
(R) Book report
(M) Math fair brochure
(W) Narrative writing

Diagrams...

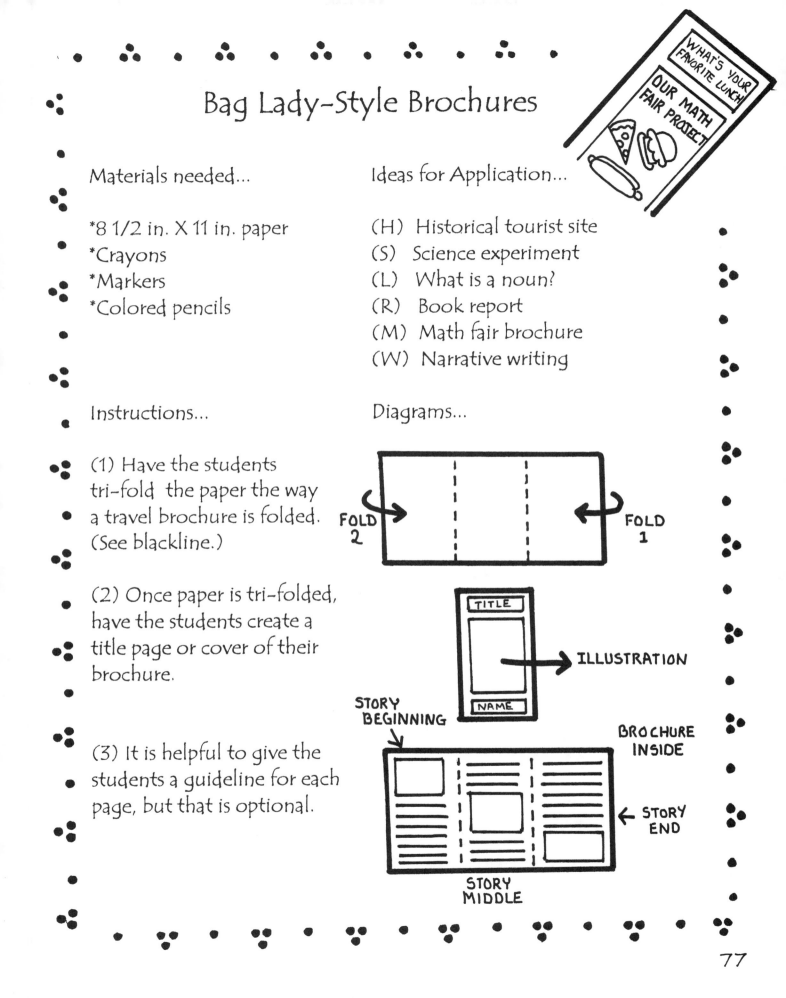

(4) Have the students write and/or illustrate their brochure. This may be done individually or in groups. This is a great project for the culminating activity of a unit or as an assessment.

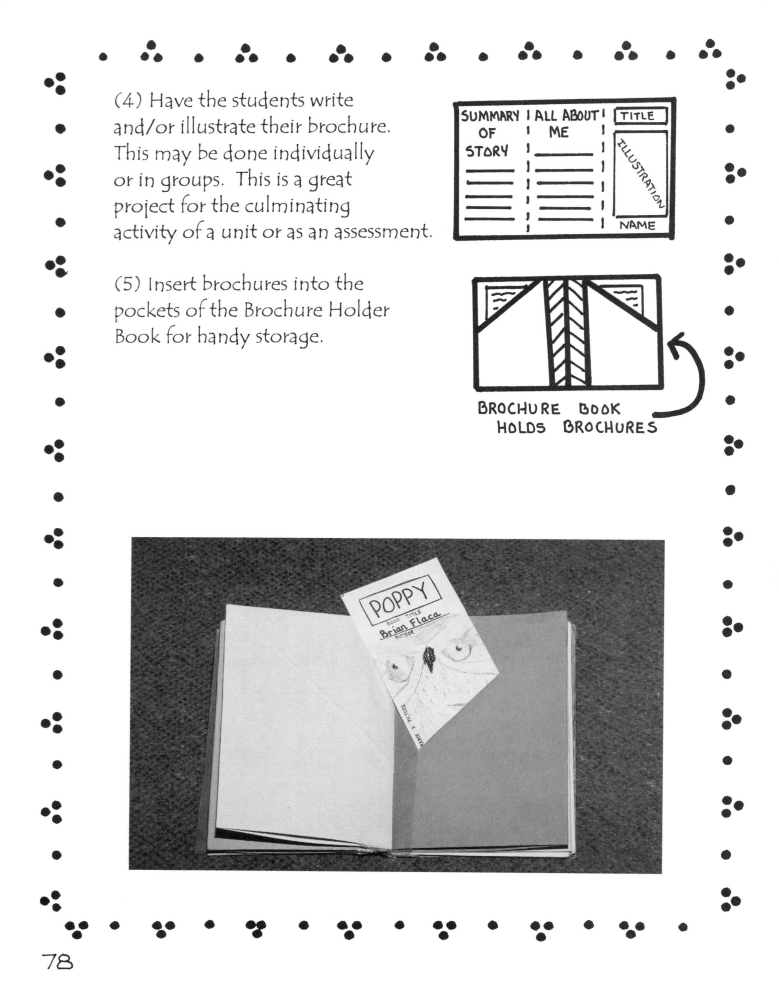

SUMMARY OF STORY	ALL ABOUT ME	TITLE
		ILLUSTRATION
		NAME

(5) Insert brochures into the pockets of the Brochure Holder Book for handy storage.

BROCHURE BOOK
HOLDS BROCHURES

POPPY
BOOK TITLE
Brian Flaca
AUTHOR

Brochure Holder Book

Materials needed...
*12 in. X 18 in. construction paper in assorted colors

Ideas for Applications...
*Great place to store brochures from previous activity.
*Store flash cards

Instructions...

Diagrams...

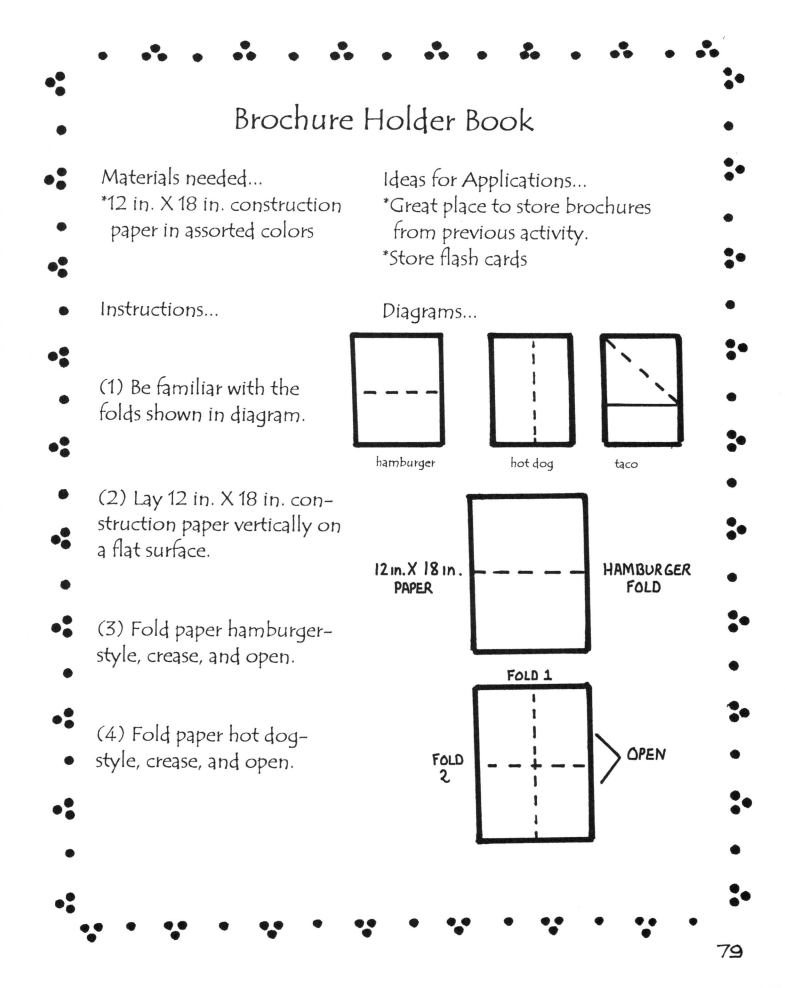

hamburger

hot dog

taco

(1) Be familiar with the folds shown in diagram.

12 in. X 18 in. PAPER

HAMBURGER FOLD

(2) Lay 12 in. X 18 in. construction paper vertically on a flat surface.

FOLD 1

(3) Fold paper hamburger-style, crease, and open.

FOLD 2

OPEN

(4) Fold paper hot dog-style, crease, and open.

(5) Fold top two corners taco style towards the center of the paper, crease, and leave folded.

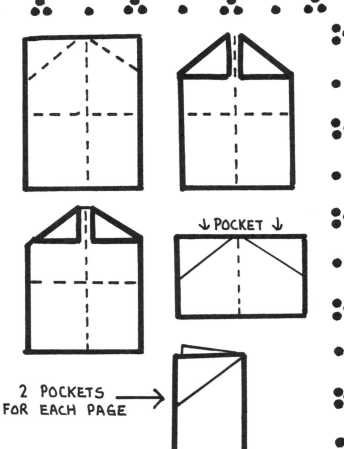

(6) Refold on the hamburger fold lines so that you cover the taco folds.

↓ POCKET ↓

(7) Refold on the hot dog fold lines.

2 POCKETS FOR EACH PAGE →

(8) Follow the Bag Lady bookbinding instructions to create a book with this style of pages. NOTE: These pages must be taped on both sides when binding to secure the pockets on both sides.

(9) Insert your brochures or flash cards.

Brochure Book
with
book reports
by
4th grade class
1999

Daily Times News

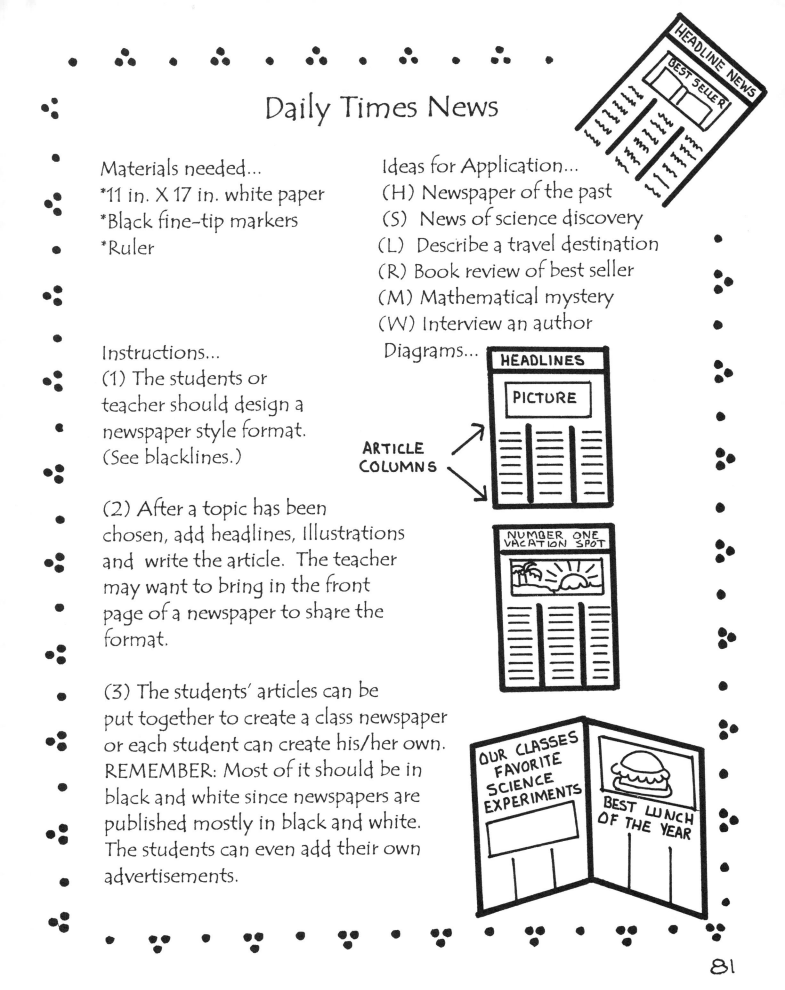

Materials needed...
* *11 in. X 17 in. white paper
* *Black fine-tip markers
* *Ruler

Instructions...

(1) The students or teacher should design a newspaper style format. (See blacklines.)

(2) After a topic has been chosen, add headlines, Illustrations and write the article. The teacher may want to bring in the front page of a newspaper to share the format.

(3) The students' articles can be put together to create a class newspaper or each student can create his/her own. REMEMBER: Most of it should be in black and white since newspapers are published mostly in black and white. The students can even add their own advertisements.

Ideas for Application...
(H) Newspaper of the past
(S) News of science discovery
(L) Describe a travel destination
(R) Book review of best seller
(M) Mathematical mystery
(W) Interview an author

Diagrams...

HEADLINE NEWS

BEST SELLER

HEADLINES

PICTURE

ARTICLE COLUMNS

NUMBER ONE VACATION SPOT

OUR CLASSES FAVORITE SCIENCE EXPERIMENTS

BEST LUNCH OF THE YEAR

Reports To Go

Material needed...
* A variety of take-out containers
* Construction paper
* Glue
* markers, crayons, or colored pencils

Ideas for Applications...
(H) Presidents to go
(S) Energy sources to go
(L) Adjectives to go
(R) Books to go
(M) Math facts to go
(W) Writing prompts to go

Instructions...

(1) The students or teacher chooses a take-out container for the reports. NOTE: It's best to use clean containers donated by various restaurants.

(2) Students will decorate the take-out box with the theme of the report.

(3) Students then create props and/or characters to go inside their containers.

Diagrams...

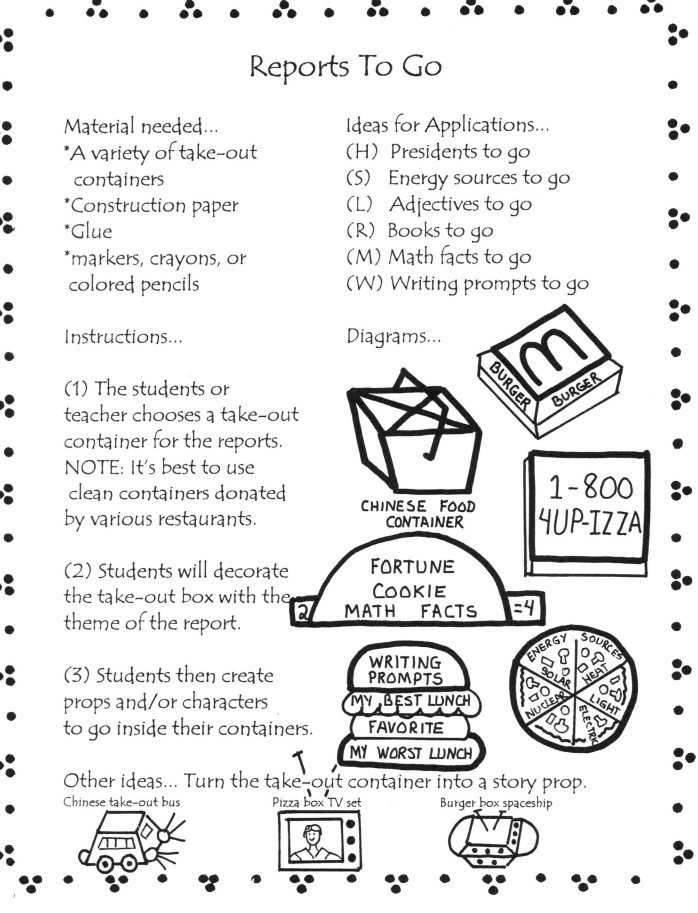

CHINESE FOOD CONTAINER

1-800 4UP-IZZA

FORTUNE COOKIE MATH FACTS

WRITING PROMPTS
MY BEST LUNCH
FAVORITE
MY WORST LUNCH

ENERGY SOURCES
SOLAR HEAT
NUCLEAR ELECTRIC LIGHT

Other ideas... Turn the take-out container into a story prop.

Chinese take-out bus   Pizza box TV set   Burger box spaceship

Overlay Story

ADD AN ITEM IN THE WINDOW OF EACH PAGE TO CREATE A COMPLETE STORY.

Materials needed...

*4 sheets 8 1/2 in. X 11 in. card stock quality paper
*Laminating film
*Scissors
*Crayons, markers, or colored pencils

Instructions...

(1) Students should first begin with illustrations and then begin their story. The first step is drawing an environment scene for the last page. (See blackline without dotted lines.)

(2) Next, complete the second to last page using the dotted line blackline master. Complete by drawing one additional item in the frame and cut the rest of the window away. The dotted lines help the students see where to draw, so pictures will be in different locations on the page.

Ideas for Applications...

(H)   Historic scene
(S)   Stages of an experiment
(L)   Expository writing
(R)   Retelling a story
(M)   Multiply step problems
(W)   Narrative writing

Diagram...

CUT AWAY ALL BUT HOUSE

(3) Repeat this process for pages 1 and 2. While students are working on these overlays they can also begin writing a rough draft for their story on paper. (We like to take the students' photos in an action pose, cut around their picture, and make it part of one of their overlays)

(4) Once all overlays are completed and story has been edited, students can transfer their story to the overlays.

(5) When completed, laminate each page and bind together. If a laminating machine is not available each page can be placed in its own page protector and then bound together.

Zipper Baggie Quilt

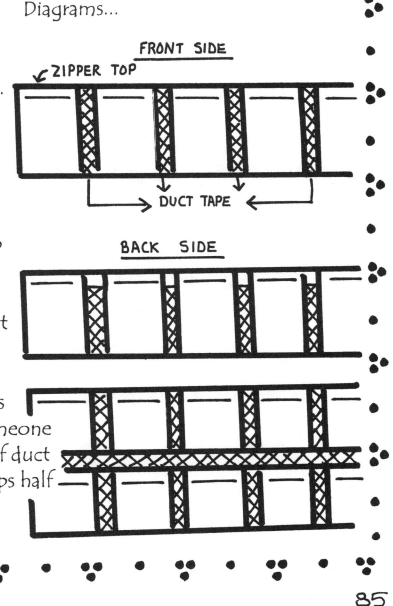

Materials needed...
* *30 zipper style baggies
  (quart size, NOT pleated)
* *Three rolls of colored
  duct tape
* *Scissors

Ideas for Application...
(H) Illustrations of explorers
(S) Animals from your state
(L) Noun/verb illustrations
(R) My favorite book
(M) Our best math work
(W) Our best writing samples

Instructions...

(1) Using duct tape, tape to-gether five rows of six baggies. To attach baggies, use one strip of duct tape running it half on one baggie and half on the other.

(2) Flip over each baggie strip (from step 1) and cover the backside of the baggie with more tape. CAUTION: do not tape over the zipper.

(3) To attach the baggie strips together it is best to have someone assist you. Run a long strip of duct tape to attach two baggie strips half the tape on each strip.

Diagrams...

FRONT SIDE
ZIPPER TOP
DUCT TAPE

BACK SIDE

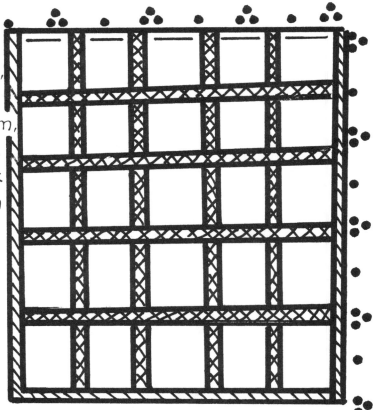

(4) After all strips are attached, run the duct tape around the left side, right side, and bottom, of the quilt (half on/half off). Fold the duct tape to the back side to create a nice border on your quilt.

(5) Insert student work through the back side, zip closed, and display.

Craft Foam Ideas

What is craft foam?

Craft foam is often sold under the brand name of FUN FOAM. It is sold in construction paper-like sheets made from a light-weight, easy-to-cut foam material. It comes in a wide variety of colors and thickness. You can write on it too.

Where do I buy craft foam?

Most craft stores carry craft foam and it can be found in the children's craft section of the store. I usually buy my craft foam from Wal-mart.

Is craft foam expensive?

No, not at all! It costs about $.35/sheet and DON'T throw any of it away; the scraps are great for projects too. We keep a box of scraps in our classrooms for all to share.

I found it, now what do I do with it?

The Bag Ladies have gone crazy with craft foam. Once you use it for one project you will think of a million other ways to use it too. Here are a few suggestions:

Visors that attach to sunglasses   Dominoes   Puzzles   Shape Books

Cameras   Tangram sets   Rubber stamps   Masks

The Memory Book of A Llama in the Family

Author: Johanna Hurwitz

A Llama in the Family
This is a story about a boy Adam thought he was going to get a bike. He was so surprised when he came home from school to see a llama. His mother had bought her him. He wasn't excited. Like no body that he loved all of his allowance. Anyway for one. He did not want Ethan Allen to be lonely so he bought another llama he spilled it so he likes her now.

This is me with my Llama Ethan Allen.

This is me when I saw my new Llama.

Chapter Five

Get your students excited about reading.
Projects of all types.

Reading

Get your students excited about reading.

"Tonight, boys and girls, when your mom or dad tells you to go to bed, I want you to take this book and this flashlight and jump into that bed and READ!" So begins another year of tricking students to read for enjoyment. "When your mom or dad opens that door and asks you what you are doing, you say, 'I'm reading!' and watch them faint!" This is one way to get your reluctant readers to buy into reading for fun. Between the two of us, we've tried them all, so here are some ways to foster reading in your classroom.

Use reading logs, which are signed every night. At the end of the month, give out books you received from your bonus points to students under different categories: most improved, most minutes, most books, etc.

Each month assign a different book presentation due at the end of the month. Begin with the cereal box covered with the report and giving the report to small groups while everyone eats the cereal in the bowls with the milk you provide. This gets them excited enough to ask, "What's next month's presentation?"

Begin all thematic units with the teacher's faaaavorite book. Soon they say, they're all your faaaavorite books! Show students how much fun books are and why. Use picture books in all grades!

Join book clubs and go over the monthly book club order, book by book. Be very excited about the books! Give out a list of your selections that you feel are the best, along with encouraging them to use their interests also. Parents love teacher selections! I use: Simmons' Selections of the Month. Your orders will double and so will your bonus points!

Make "glasses"with your students from two circles of a six-pack ring and/or pipecleaners. Have everyone wear his/her glasses to read.

Read to your class every day! Choose a novel that you and your class can enjoy and do projects with. Usually I choose a book that goes with my theme at the time or just an author whose book I want to read. I try to read with great expression and have found that the students will try to mimic my reading when they read!

In intermediate or late primary grades, after choosing a novel that the group is reading, read a chapter each day. You, the teacher, read all the narration and the students read all the parts of the characters. This reader's theater-type reading is what we have found to be the biggest asset to our readers in motivation and expression. We advocate the use of all methods of reading for enjoyment and understanding, silent, partner, group, etc., but this method really excites the students to want to read more and read on in the novel, and isn't that what our goal is, along with strengthening skills?

If the video is available for the book you are reading, the class loves to see the chapters that they have read each week, so every Friday we watch the parts of the story we have read. Most of the time at the end of the story, students will agree that they enjoyed the book better than the video.

In our quest to "read between the lines" and find the ideal way to get students to love reading and to practice reading, we have found that no one method works but the combination of many encouraging, exciting, methods with, of course, projects to motivate them.

Included next is a list of favorite authors and/or books that we enjoy using with our themes.

BAG LADIES' FAVORITES.......BOOKS AND AUTHORS

It makes us laugh to even list our favorite books because we have a new favorite book every week!   Every time we share a book with our students we tell them it's our favorite book EVER! They say, "Boy, you have a lot of favorite books!" And we proudly answer, "We sure DO!" We purchase so many books that we have to do it cheaply. Therefore we use our book clubs extensively and discount book stores make a great rainy day trip! Sometimes we fall so deeply in love with a certain book that we have to have our own. We don't know about you, but we have trouble sharing that "favorite" book, so we make it a point to buy each other her own copy!

In almost all of our workshops, participants will ask us for a bibliography of books that we use in our units. These books are listed in each of our separate units as to themes but we are going to attempt to give you a list of just some of our favorite books to use with any age depending on your theme. So here goes...These are the books that we own our own copy of.

A River Ran Wild, by Lynne Cherry; _Wump World_, by Bill Peet; _The Hundred Penny Box_, by Sharon Bell Mathis; _Mirette on the High Wire_ , (and the sequel) by Emily Arnold; _The Pink Motel_ , by Carol Ryrie Brink; _Everglades_, by Jean Craighead George; _Jolly Mon_, by Savannah and Jimmy Buffett; _Green Wilma_, by Tedd Arnold; _Antics_, by Cathi Hepworth; _Stellaluna_, by Janell Cannon; _A Street Called Home_, by Aminah Brenna Lynn Robinson; _Two Bad Ants_, by Chris Van Allsburg; _Wartville Wizard_, by Don Madden; _Sadako and the 1000 Paper Cranes_, by Eleanor Coerr;

It Looked Like Spilled Milk, by Charles G.Shaw; _The Lion, the Witch, and the Wardobe_, by C.S.Lewis; _The Grouchy Ladybug_, by Eric Carle;

Holes, by Louis Sachar; _Counting on Frank_, by Rod Clement; _Jolly Postman_ books, by Janet and Allen Ahlberg; _Amelia's Notebook_, (and sequels) by Marissa Moss; _Quick as a Cricket_, by Audrey Woods;

Tar Beach, by Faith Ringgold; _The Keeping Quilt_, by Patricia Polacco;

Chrysanthemum, by Kevin Henkes; _A Chair for my Mother_, by Vera B. Williams; _The Lion's Paw_, by Robb White; _Beach Feet_, by Lynn Reisner;

The Greatest Table, by Michael Rosen; _Hooray for Diffendoofer Day_, by Jack Prelutsky and Lane Smith; _How to Hide a Butterfly_, by Ruth Heller;

The Apron, by Eric Carle; _Did You Carry the Flag Today, Charlie_, by Rebecca Caudill; _A Pigtale_, by Olivia Newton John; and.....of course,

many many more.

   We have mentioned SOME of our favorite books from our thematic units. As we write new units we add more books to this list. It's a neverending cycle and is the basis for all of the units that we teach! Our goal is for students always to be as excited about reading as we are! Enjoy, and add your own "favorites."

Eyeglasses

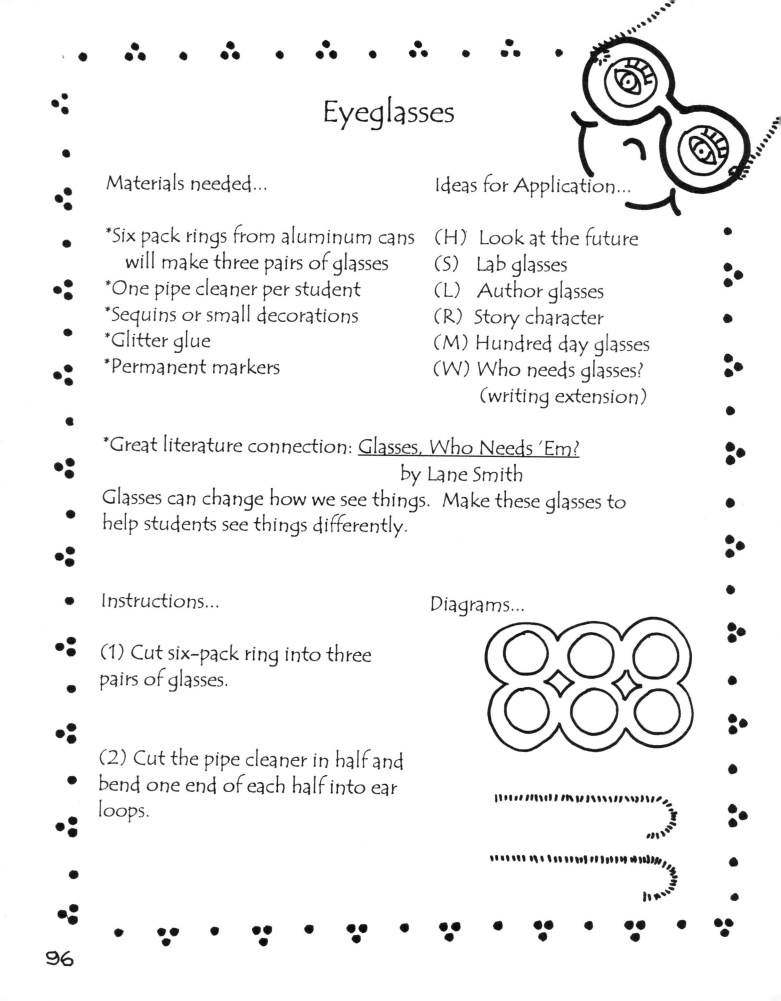

Materials needed...

*Six pack rings from aluminum cans will make three pairs of glasses
*One pipe cleaner per student
*Sequins or small decorations
*Glitter glue
*Permanent markers

*Great literature connection: <u>Glasses, Who Needs 'Em?</u>
by Lane Smith
Glasses can change how we see things. Make these glasses to help students see things differently.

Ideas for Application...

(H) Look at the future
(S) Lab glasses
(L) Author glasses
(R) Story character
(M) Hundred day glasses
(W) Who needs glasses?
        (writing extension)

Instructions...

(1) Cut six-pack ring into three pairs of glasses.

(2) Cut the pipe cleaner in half and bend one end of each half into ear loops.

Diagrams...

(3) Hole punch one hole on each side of six-pack ring.

HOLE PUNCH

(4) Insert pipe cleaners and twist to secure through each hole punch.

(5) Your eyeglasses are now ready to be decorated with sequins, glitter glue, etc.

Pipe Cleaner Eyeglasses...

Materials needed...

*Four pipe cleaners per pair
   (bright, jazzy colors are best)
*Scissors

Instructions...   Diagrams...

(1) Choose two pipe cleaners to be the frames and loop them into desired shape.

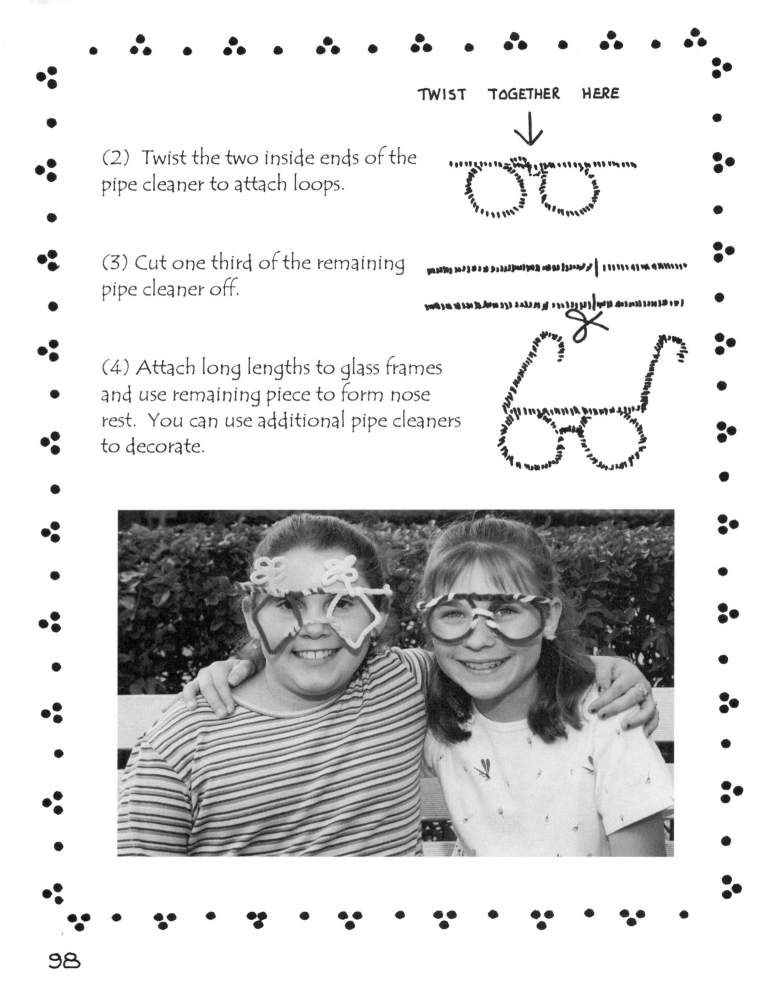

TWIST TOGETHER HERE

(2) Twist the two inside ends of the pipe cleaner to attach loops.

(3) Cut one third of the remaining pipe cleaner off.

(4) Attach long lengths to glass frames and use remaining piece to form nose rest. You can use additional pipe cleaners to decorate.

Story Aprons

Materials needed...

*One tall white unpleated garbage bag per two students. This can also be made from wallpaper, fabric, or butcher paper.

*Scissors

*Permanent markers

Instructions...

(1) Cut tall garbage bags in half vertically.

(2) Follow the diagram in drawing the apron on the bag. For younger students, draw the pattern on tagboard and then onto the bag.

(3) Cut along lines on the drawing, cutting through both layers of the bag. When cut and opened, the bag will look like the diagram.

(4) Decorate the apron to go along with the theme. If using white garbage bags, permanent markers work best. With butcher paper or wallpaper, regular markers and crayons work fine.

Ideas for Application...

(H) Thanksgiving apron

(S) Science lab apron

(L) How-to story apron

(R) Reading log apron

(M) Measurements apron

(W) Author's apron

Diagrams...

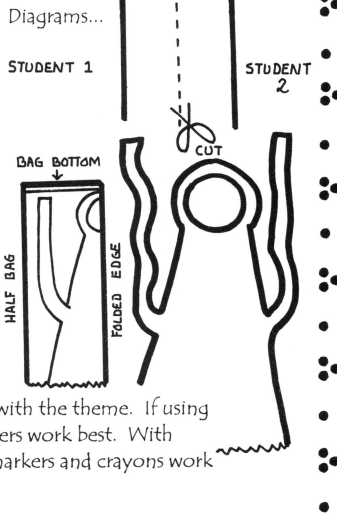

MY FAVORITE AUTHOR, BOOK TITLES, & ILLUSTRATIONS

STUDENT 1

STUDENT 2

CUT

BAG BOTTOM

HALF BAG

FOLDED EDGE

Cereal Box Projects

Materials needed...

* Cereal box, any size
* 2 sheets white paper
  11 in. X 17 in.
* colored pencils, markers,
  and crayons
* Scissors

Instructions...

(1) Have each person or group
bring in one box of cereal (we
tell our students they can bring
a full box or a partially filled box).

(2) Each student or group
chooses a topic for the box
and covers it with paper.

(3) Group or student decides what
information will appear on the box,
cut it out, illustrate with headings,
facts, drawings.

Ideas for Application...

(H) Historical event box
(S) Good nutrition box
(L) Description box
(R) Book report box
(M) Fraction cereal box
(W) Field trip in a box

Diagrams...

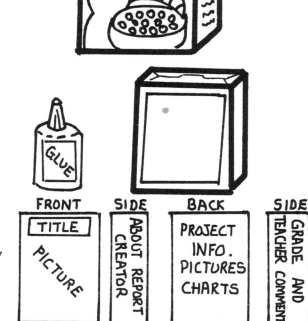

Bring in bowls, spoons, and milk, and watch students share reports while they eat!

GUIDED READING AT-HOME LOG

FOR _____

DATE	BOOK READ	READ TO	PAGES	PARENT'S SIGNATURE

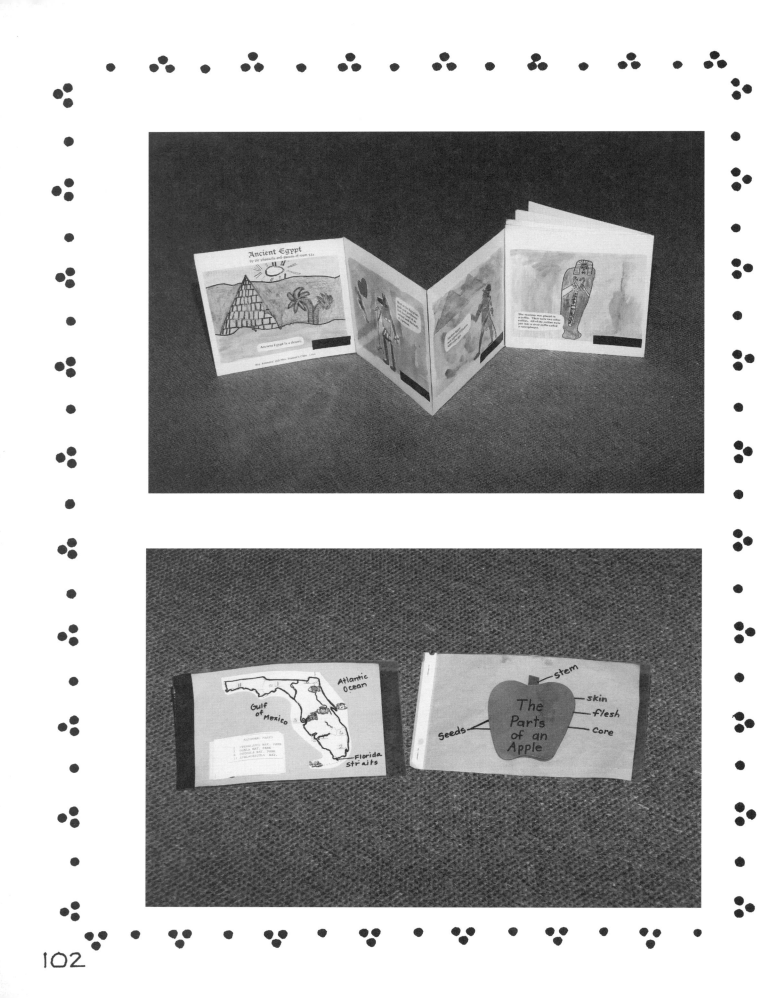

Chapter Six

Tips for teachers that add up to a successful classroom.
Portfolio conferences and everything to go with them.

Math

Tips for teachers that "add up" to a successful classroom.

Part of our job as educators is to bring our parents into the classroom to see where their child began the year, where he/she is going, and again at the end of the year to view the progress made. We do this with a variety of portfolio conferences during the last 20 minutes of the day. These are conferences strictly between the student and the parent. An invitation is sent home and part of the invitation is sent back as the RSVP. (Examples follow.) Most parents will strive to come in, especially when the return says, "No, I cannot attend the conference, please secure another partner for my child." If the parent cannot make the meeting, ask a speech teacher, ESE teacher, or principal to attend. These are short but very informative conferences for anyone who attends. The children are scripted and do a lovely job of greeting their parents/guests and taking them to their seat to view, read, and/or solve problems depending on whether it is a writing portfolio conference or a math journal conference. (Scripts follow.) Also, serve something small that the students can prepare at the end of their conference or plan a group presentation to conclude the event. Parents will sign comment sheets about their experience at the "party." Parties are usually thematic in nature to go with the classroom theme, decorations, and costumes. For example, while studying Florida, students dressed as Florida tourists with visors, fanny packs, (made from paper and watercolored), and cameras.

They served cheeseburgers in paradise: two vanilla wafers, a peppermint patty in between, with a dab of colored frosting (green, yellow, and red) to depict the condiments. Squeeze together and enjoy! Take pictures of this event and post on your Web site or in the room.

Another great way to get parents into the classroom is to turn the room into a period of history or a state or civilization. After the room is completely decorated wall to wall with artifacts, posters, etc., parents are invited to "tour" the area with their costumed child as the tour guide. Parents are amazed at their child's knowledge of the material, and you find this hands-on method to work for even your most hard-to-learn student. Plus, your room looks fabulous!

You can buy so many materials now that go with different themes that your bulletin boards come alive even before the first day of school.

For Mother's Day, a great idea is a Mother's Day Tea. Students can read their portfolios to their moms while they serve "tea" and cookies. Buy mugs from garage sales during the year, and every mom will go home with a mug of her own. Students can make hats from newspaper for each mom before they come to the party. Other portfolio ideas and invitation suggestions follow, along with the script that our students use in any grade, and a comment sheet for the guest to fill out each time you host a portfolio party. Remember, these parties can be for any subject in which you want your students to show where they have started and their growth in that area.

Newspaper Hats

Materials needed...

*Three full-size sheets
  of newspaper
*2 in. wide masking
  tape
*Scissors (optional)
*Decorations for hats

Instructions...

(1) Students should work in
groups of three.
Student 1-head mold
Student 2-designer
Student 3-tape cutter
Lay three open sheets of
newspaper on Student 1.

(2) Using masking tape, go
around and around
(approximately three times)
Student 1's head and create
a hat brim

Ideas for Applications...

(H) Red, white, and blue hats
(S) Recycling hats
(L) Get creative hats
(R) Story character hats
(M) Math manipulative hats
(W) Author's hats

Diagrams...

107

(3) Roll up the bottom of the newspaper to form a rim for the hat. Tape cutter (Student 3) should tear or cut 1 in. slices of tape for the designer and tape the rim into place.

TAPE →

TOP VIEW
OF HAT

(4) Hats can then be spray painted, covered with tissue paper, and/or decorated with flowers, feathers, ribbons, pom-poms, etc.

Portfolio conferences and everything to go with them.

Mother's Day Tea-Buy mugs at garage sales, $.05 each, and invite moms
to the class so students can share their best work. Make a poem
book for moms to take home.

Classroom Museum/Art Show-Students are the tour guides for whatever your theme is and parents are the tourists! Students can
copy the "masters" artwork and even sell their creations.

Recycling Picnic-Hot dogs, lemonade, and recycling work together
while students show their portfolios and make rubber stamps.

Paradise Party-Everyone dresses like a Florida tourist with visors,
fanny packs, and cameras. Play tropical music and eat
"cheeseburgers in paradise."

I Love the U.S.A.-Wear red, white, and blue. Serve apple pie and sing
patriotic songs.

Garden Party-Dress in your Sunday best. Tablecloths, flowers, and
finger foods.

Books-and-Breakfast-Students bring in different varieties of cereal.
Guests eat cereals while listening to book talks which are on
cereal boxes.

Cocoa-and-Conversation-Discuss portfolios while drinking cocoa and
eating cookies.

Author's Tea- Discuss portfolios over tea and biscuits, Oprah book club
style.

Mathsquerade Party- Happy Mardi Gras. Students celebrate with
student-made math games and guests. Make masks and beads!

Portfolio party invitations

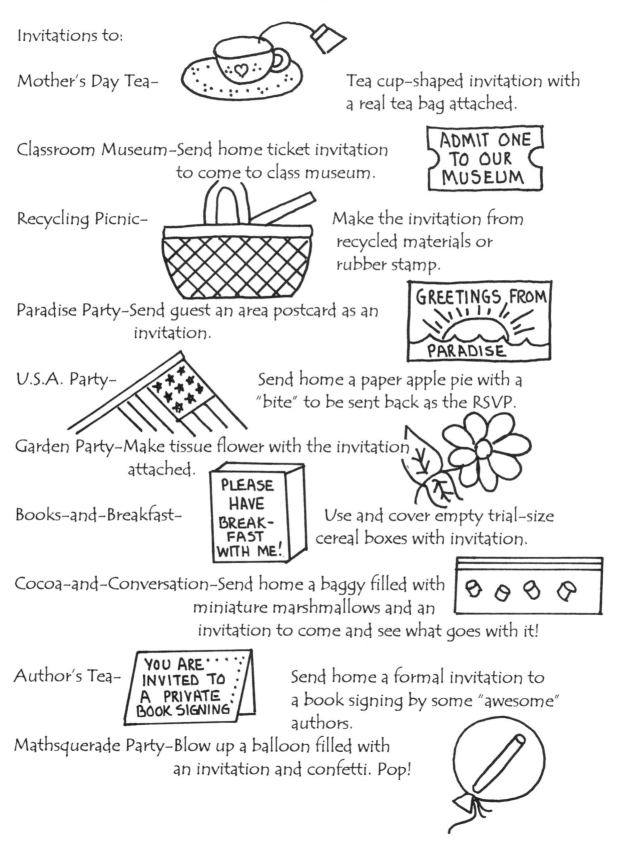

Invitations to:

Mother's Day Tea- Tea cup-shaped invitation with a real tea bag attached.

Classroom Museum-Send home ticket invitation to come to class museum.

ADMIT ONE TO OUR MUSEUM

Recycling Picnic- Make the invitation from recycled materials or rubber stamp.

Paradise Party-Send guest an area postcard as an invitation.

GREETINGS FROM PARADISE

U.S.A. Party- Send home a paper apple pie with a "bite" to be sent back as the RSVP.

Garden Party-Make tissue flower with the invitation attached.

Books-and-Breakfast-

PLEASE HAVE BREAK-FAST WITH ME!

Use and cover empty trial-size cereal boxes with invitation.

Cocoa-and-Conversation-Send home a baggy filled with miniature marshmallows and an invitation to come and see what goes with it!

Author's Tea-

YOU ARE INVITED TO A PRIVATE BOOK SIGNING

Send home a formal invitation to a book signing by some "awesome" authors.

Mathsquerade Party-Blow up a balloon filled with an invitation and confetti. Pop!

Portfolio Party Agenda

Student greets guest at the door when student sees the guest arrive.

Student says, " Thank you (Mom, or Dad, etc.) for coming to my conference. I know you are busy and had to leave work to come."

Student seats guest in student's seat at student's desk.

Student presents portfolio. "This is my writing portfolio. Do you know what expository and narrative stories are? I will explain them to you, and I will show you some examples of my first stories and how I am writing now."

Student reads first story and compares it to newer stories.

Student reads something special that he/she made for the party or his or her favorite writing along with any favorite writing projects.

Student asks guest to fill in conference comment sheet.

Student then serves treat or tours the room with the guest.

HELPFUL HINTS

Send home written invitations with RSVP to come back.

Practice conferencing with another class. If a girl comes to the door, it is your mom. A boy is your dad.

Limit party time to less than 30 minutes.

Secure substitutes for absentee parents: aides, volunteers, speech tchr., ESE tchr.,

Videotape the party or take lots of pictures for later projects.

Stick to the agenda. No conferences with the teacher, only child-parent.

Portfolio party costumes

Mother's Day Tea-Wear your Sunday best.

Classroom Museum-Dress to go with museum theme. Egyptian museum togas and Egyptian collars

Recycling Picnic-Picnic clothes, picnic baskets

Paradise Party-Tourist T-shirts, visors, sunglasses, fanny pack, camera

U.S.A. Party-Newspaper hats and red, white, and blue clothing

Garden Party-Gardening hats, overalls, gardening gloves

Books-and-Breakfast-Robes and slippers

Cocoa-and-Conversation-Mittens, scarves, and ski caps

Author's Tea-Author's apron

Mathsquerade Party-Mask on a dowel rod with curling ribbon, beads

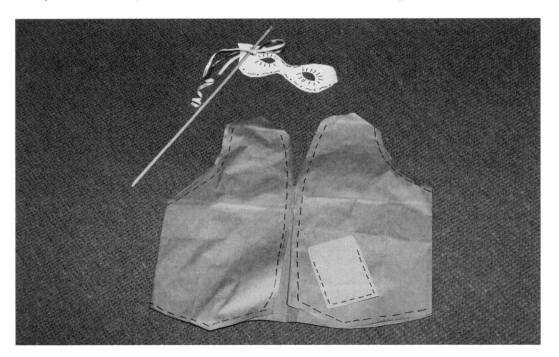

Portfolio Conference Comment Sheet

For_____on_____

Guest_____

    Please comment on the presentation of the portfolio conference and the writing that you have observed.

_____

_____

_____

_____

_____

_____

_____

- -

Portfolio Conference Comment Sheet

For_____on_____

Guest_____

    Please comment on the presentation of the portfolio conference and the writing that you have observed.

_____

_____

_____

_____

_____

_____

_____

Chapter Seven

Now it's your turn to write a
thematic unit: Here's how.

Writing Thoughts
with the
Bag Ladies

TEACHING MATERIALS FOR
TEACHERS

Writing

Now it's your turn to write a thematic unit: Here's how.

We can hear you say, "I do that!" or "I can do that!" We can't tell you how many workshops we attend where we say the same thing. And the answer is, "Of course, you can!" As teachers we have all had a hand in writing, re-creating, or supplementing classroom units. Now, join us in a step-by-step guaranteed fail-safe method of writing your own thematic unit. This unit will be geared specifically to your classroom objectives, grade level, and ideas (please steal some of ours). CONGRATULATIONS! You are on your way to getting excited about teaching, your way, with the Bag Ladies to guide you there.

One last tip and probably the most important one of all: Find a partner-someone who has some of the same teaching philosophies that you do, wants to be excited about teaching in a "hands-on" classroom, and is willing to brainstorm and share both ideas and expenses in order to plan together. We can't stress enough how much the adage "Two heads are better than one" applies here. Ideas seem to feed off of each other as the two of you are brainstorming, it makes planning so much more fun, and therefore the job is creative with less work.

Choose your partner or two, get a large container to hold all of your ideas and models, and pick a theme that you are interested in. Now go looking for some great literature in picture books and novels that you can't resist. Oh, and maybe buy two of the books, one for you and one for your partner. We used to share new books we found. Have you ever tried to share books that you use in your classroom? It never worked for us! We learned to just buy two and save ourselves a lot of aggravation.

Look for the books on "reduced and clearance shelves" or at our favorite places to buy books, Target or Wal-Mart. Many of you also have "teacher book/supply stores" with excellent sales people who can guide you into new and/or great literature to go with your themes. Also, please note that we use the curriculum/textbooks given to us by our district as part of our resources, a very important part. It is the addition to this, though, that in many ways will make your unit exciting for you to teach and for your students to be motivated!

We can tell that you are ready to start. Browse through the next few pages and you are off to writing a great new thematic unit!

Bag Ladies' 12 Steps to a Great Unit

Step 1......................Choose a theme

Step 2......................Organize resources

Step 3......................Create a web plan

Step 4......................Plan your projects

Step 5......................List your benchmarks

Step 6......................Skill activities for the
          pocket chart

Step 7......................Vocabulary lists

Step 8......................Graphic organizers

Step 9......................Planning calendar

Step 10....................Assessing your unit
          and your students

Step 11....................Portfolio party plan

Step 12....................Evaluate your unit

Step 1.Choose a theme

You can take almost any topic and turn it into a theme. Things to consider are your students' interests, your grade level objective, and the integration of the theme into multiple subject areas. Remember, be specific, don't just say animals is your theme, pick a category like ocean mammals. Here's our brainstorm of ideas.

Colors-Five Senses-Animals-Insects-Imaginary creatures-My state
Native Americans-Environmental Habitats-State Parks-Birds
Famous Americans-Famous explorers-Sport teams-Endangered
animals-Plants-Caves-Grasshoppers-Crickets-Bears-Frogs-n-toads,
Animal life cycle-Ants-Bees-Butterflies-Moths-Worms-Reptiles
Amphibians-Nocturnal animals-Colonial times-Vacation planning
in the U.S.A-Conflict resolution-Choose a state-American sports,
American folklore-Kites-Clouds-Weather-Space transportation
Chocolate-Early civilizations-Dinosaurs-Africa-Ancient Egypt,
Egypt now-Gods and Goddesses-Earth Day-Trees-Seasons-Spiders
Quilts-Energy-Ecosystems-Biomes-Nutrition-Ponds and lakes,
Oceans-Ocean animals-Ocean mammals-Wildlife-Families-Shapes,
Patterns-Fabrics-Cotton-Autobiographies-Family trees-Inventions,
Inventors-Black Americans-Countries of the world-Folktales,
Tall tales-Fairy tales-Safari-Australia-Arctic regions-Cultural
diversity-Multi-cultural celebration-Rainforest-Poetry-Eggs,
Things under the ground-Things on the ground-Things in the
air-My community-Occupations-Presidents-A trip around the
world-Pen pals-Famous artists-Famous musicians-Manners,
Poetry-Choose a favorite author-Foreign languages-Pets,
The islands-Geography-Map reading and making-Bookmaking
Classroom publishing-Math carnival-Recycling-Friendship,
Life in America 100 years ago-Life in America in 100 years.
Now it's your turn to think of some topics that would make a
great unit! Have fun.

Step 2. Organize resources

*Choosing the topic books-If you are using picture books, we like to use approximately one each day that a new part of the unit is introduced. Don't forget older students love picture books and children of all ages like to hear the same good book more than once.

      Example: Sea mammals
            manatees-*Sammy the Sea Cow*
            dolphins-*Jolly Mon*

Be sure to list the book titles, the author, and where you got the book (school library, public library, or borrowed from_____). We find that it is good to own those SPECIAL stories and others are fine just to borrow from the library, so pick and choose before you go and buy every book on your list.

*Featured author-We like to choose between two and four authors to feature for each unit. This is our chance to share other books by an author that don't fit into this or any other units we have planned. You can use these authors stories and illustrations as a guide for student publications.

*Music, Art, P.E, and Cooking-This is the part that really grabs the students. Let the students bring in music and recipes to go along with the theme. We like to keep the cooking simple...blue Jello with gummy fish is a great treat for an ocean unit.

*Bulletin boards-Don't spend night and day making bulletin boards for your classroom. They look just as good covered in theme-related fabric and you can use them to display the students' work. You can make one centerpiece item until the students have work to be put up.

121

*Skills I will cover during this unit-Choose four main skills you would like to cover during this unit, in different subject areas if possible. For example, Math-measurements, Science-shadows, Language Arts-commas in a series, Social Studies-time zones and seasons around the world.

*Projects-Choose four projects from the ones we have given you or think of some of your own. Don't plan too many projects; remember, quality over quantity. Start with four projects and add more if needed later.

*Materials-What kinds of materials and supplies do you need to collect for your unit? Do yourself a favor and list everything on your resource page so next time you do this unit you have a ready-made shopping list. We like to make a list of everything we need and only go on one shopping trip at the beginning of our unit, that way we're not running to the craft store every week for just one more thing. Examples: craft foam, pipe cleaners, and paints

*Helpful hints for next time-Add to this column throughout the unit. List any changes you would make and anything that would make things go easier next time.

*Now it's your turn to plan a unit! Make copies of the blacklines in this chapter. We find it is easiest to copy these blackline masters on to 11 in. X 17 in. copy paper and enlarge them. That will give you plenty of room to write. The Bag Ladies then store their unit in handy handled bags but, file folders will work just as well.

READY............................SET...PLAN

RESOURCE PAGE

CHOOSE A TOPIC-MAKE IT CATCHY

TOPIC BOOKS-AUTHORS	MORE TOPIC BOOKS-AUTHORS	FEATURED AUTHORS
MUSIC-ART-P.E.-COOKING	BULLETIN BOARDS IDEAS	SKILLS TO BE COVERED
PROJECTS	MATERIALS NEEDED	HELPFUL HINTS FOR NEXT TIME…

123

STEP 3.Create a web plan

Organize your activities on a planning web so you are sure to hit all subject areas. Creating a web before filling in your Planning calendar (Step 9) is a great way to organize your activities by subject area.

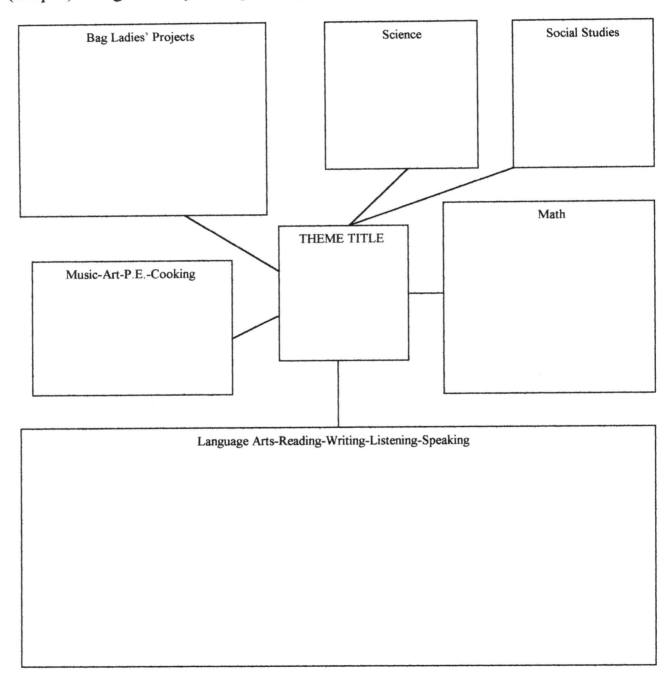

Step 4.Plan your projects

Choose four projects to start your unit; you can always add more later. Remember, variety is very important so don't use the same type of project in every unit. The students will get bored and so will you. We like to start a project at the beginning of each week and wrap it up by the end of the week.

Project 1_____Page Number____
Supplies needed / Subject Area / Special Instructions / Notes and changes...

Project 2_____Page Number____
Supplies needed / Subject Area / Special Instructions / Notes and changes...

Project 3_____Page Number____
Supplies needed / Subject Area / Special Instructions / Notes and changes...

Project 4_____Page Number____
Supplies needed / Subject Area / Special Instructions / Notes and changes...

My Project Ideas

Materials needed...

* _____
* _____
* _____
* _____
* _____
* _____

Instructions...

(1)_____

_____

_____

_____

(2)_____

_____

_____

_____

(3)_____

_____

_____

_____

(4)_____

_____

_____

_____

Ideas for Applications...

(H) _____
(S) _____
(L) _____
(R) _____
(M) _____
(W) _____

Diagrams...

Step 5. List your benchmarks, strategies, objectives, and skills

Use this page to list your subject area objectives. By putting all your objectives on one page at the beginning of your unit you can easily transfer them into your lesson planbook. I like to slide my objective sheet into a plastic page protector and just clip it inside of my planbook.

Math: _____

_____

Reading: _____

_____

Writing: _____

_____

Listening: _____

_____

Speaking: _____

_____

Science: _____

_____

Social Studies: _____

_____

Other: _____

_____

_____

Step 6. Skill activities for the pocket chart

When the Bag Ladies first got their pocket charts we thought they were really great but we weren't sure how we were going to use them. That was what sparked us to include a list of ideas in the units that we create. Now we have so many uses for them we have them hanging all around our classroom in all shapes and sizes. Have fun with our list of ideas and add your own.

Skill Ideas...

Sentence structure	Contractions	Clocks & times
Possessives	Vocabulary	Word meanings
Antonyms	Story starters	Spelling strategies
Writing addresses	Prefixes	Suffixes
Parts of a letter	Nouns	Rhyming words
Report writing steps	Verbs	Important facts
Punctuation	Patterning	Poetry
Word wall	Adjectives	Homographs
Homophones	Proper nouns	Compound words
Paragraph format	Similes	Vivid description
Commas in a series	Classify items	Quotation marks
Sequence	Main idea	Alliteration

Diagrams...

Eye inside and out	Life cycles of ants, bees, or butterflies
Plant parts	Parts of a vehicle, hot air balloon
Insect parts	Calendar activities

Or play games....Jeopardy, Concentration, tic-tac-toe.

Design your Pocket Chart activities

Now it's your turn...decide what lessons you want to teach using your pocket chart. Purchase index cards for vocabulary words and sentence strips for your skills. Write up practice sentences and words, laminate them, and they can be used year after year. You can also write on them with a washable marker and wipe them off so they are reusable.

Skill:_____

Practice:

Step 7. Vocabulary lists

*Theme vocabulary words should be displayed on word walls and/or in pocket charts.

*Index cards and sentence strips work well to display your vocabulary words.

*The students should help to brainstorm the vocabulary words to go with the theme and the teacher can write them on chart paper.

*As students read theme-related books they can keep a list of words that they don't know how to spell or what the words mean.

*The teacher or students can then make illustrations of the word meanings to hang in the classroom.

*Students can also make an individual vocabulary log to be kept in their portfolios, and to refer to it throughout the unit.

My Theme_____

Vocabulary List   _____   _____

_____   _____   _____

_____   _____   _____

_____   _____   _____

_____   _____   _____

_____   _____   _____

_____   _____   _____

_____   _____   _____

_____   _____   _____

Step 8. Graphic organizers

*Graphic organizers are a great way to create a picture of information.

*Younger students should do graphs on chart paper as a large group at first, and then move on to individual graphs.

*Older students should learn how to chart the information, add titles, and eventually chart their information. They should also learn to transfer information from one type of graph to another type of graph.

*Graphic organizers are a great way to connect math and science into any literature selection.

*It's a good idea to show students the same information on different types of graphs and allow plenty of chances to verbalize the information on the graphs.

Suggested uses for graphs...

Venn Diagram	Bar Graph	Circle Graph
Flowering/ Plants with Plants / Fruits & Veggies	The number of states you have visited	Our favorite sports
Penguins / Pelicans	Sort & graph Sports cards	Time spent per day on different activities
Cumulus Cirrus clouds / clouds	Favorite vacation destination	How do you get to school
Frogs / Toads		
Butterflies / Moths	Methods of travel car-airplane-boat-train	Sorting foods Examples: candies or snack foods
A camera / the eye		

VENN DIAGRAMS

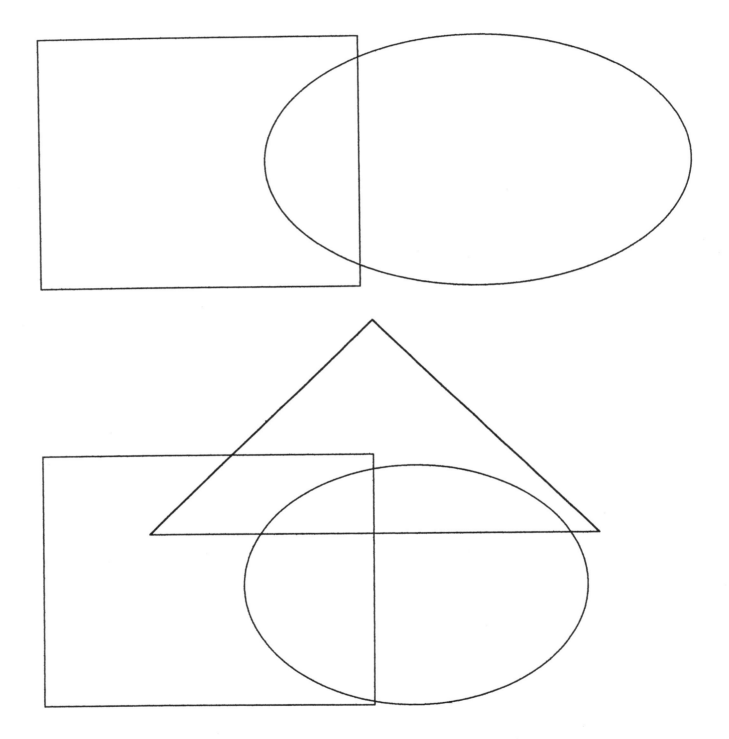

Bar Graphs/Line Graphs

_____

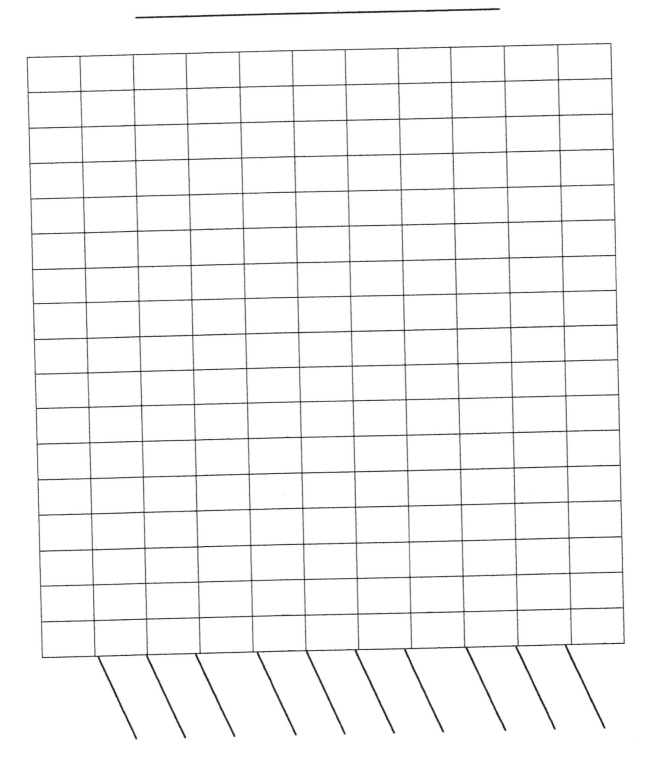

CIRCLE GRAPHS

CIRCLE GRAPH KEY:

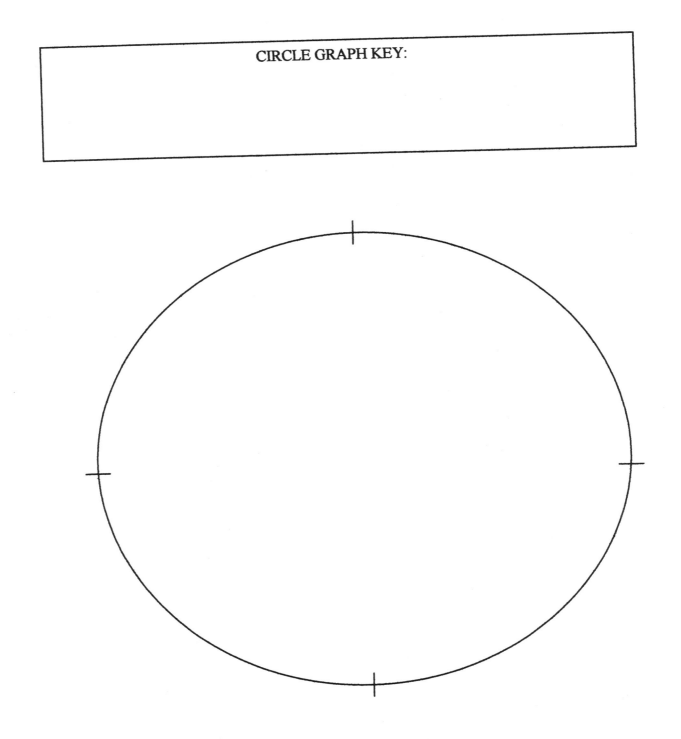

STEP 9. Planning Calendar

Put all planned activities on a calendar as a long-term plan. Four weeks is a good amount of time to spend on a unit. Don't let even the best unit drag on, and on, and on, and on.

Week	MONDAY	TUESDAY	WEDNESDAY	THURSDAY	FRIDAY
1					
2					
3					
4					

135

Step 10. Assessing your unit and students

Assessing your students on a weekly basis is very important even when teaching a theme. If you get in the habit of assessing your students weekly you will always have a running record of their progress. We find when teaching themes it is easiest to assess your students through a cumulative project, a checklist, or a rubric.

When choosing a cumulative project, choose something that will show as much about a student's newly acquired knowledge as possible. Many projects in this book lend themselves nicely as a final project that can be assessed. The following is a list of some of our favorites.

Great projects for student assessment...
* Pop-Up Book
* Seed Packet
* Scrapbook
* Filmstrip
*Brown Bag Presentations
*Brochures
*Daily News

The following pages are examples of a checklist-style assessment. They are used to assess students throughout the unit and placed in their portfolios. After the unit is completed the teacher can give students one final grade on the unit by referring to the checklist. This is an excellent way to keep track of a student's progress throughout the unit.

Another way to assess students' thematic progress is using a rubric. These rubrics are designed to be used either by the teacher or students. When using a rubric with younger students we suggest a 3-to-5 point scale, while older students can be assessed on a 10-point scale. We have included samples of Writing and Listener's Rubrics as a guide to creating your own.

Checklist Assessment Sheet

Student's Name_____

Name of Theme_____

<u>Teacher Assessments...</u>

___Reads/Comprehends Material

___Listens/Responds to groups/individuals

___Gives oral presentations clearly

___Researches assigned topic

___Reads about a topic

___Writing Activities
    ___Letter Writing
    ___Vocabulary
    ___Poetry
    ___Personal Narrative
    ___Literature Response
    ___Journal Writing

<u>Projects...</u>

___#1_____

___**#2**_____

___**#3**_____

___**#4**_____

<u>Unit Assessments...</u>

___ #1_____

___#2_____

___#3_____

___#4 Final Assessment

<u>Extra Credit...</u>

___#1_____

___#2_____

___#3_____

<u>Teacher Comments...</u>

137

Teacher Observations

Comments on...

Individual Work_____

_____

_____

Group Participation _____

_____

_____

Extra Credit _____

_____

_____

Other Activities_____

_____

_____

_____

_____

Rubric Examples

Writer's Rubric-Narrative Format

1. The writer focuses on the prompt.
   0   1   2   3   4   5   6   7   8   9   10
2. Reader is hooked by the story introduction.
   0   1   2   3   4   5   6   7   8   9   10
3. The format of the writing shows a beginning, middle, and end.
   0   1   2   3   4   5   6   7   8   9   10
4. Proper sentence structure with mechanics is used.
   0   1   2   3   4   5   6   7   8   9   10
5. Uses descriptive vocabulary with dialogue and similes.
   0   1   2   3   4   5   6   7   8   9   10

Writer's Rubric-Expository Format

1. The writer focuses on the prompt.
   0   1   2   3   4   5   6   7   8   9   10
2. Reader is hooked on the story introduction.
   0   1   2   3   4   5   6   7   8   9   10
3. The format shows grade level appropriate expectation.
   0   1   2   3   4   5   6   7   8   9   10
4. Proper sentence structure with mechanics is used.
   0   1   2   3   4   5   6   7   8   9   10
5. Numerous details are given for each reason stated.
   0   1   2   3   4   5   6   7   8   9   10

Presentation Rubric

Directions:

1. Give each student a copy of the rubric blackline master.
2. Discuss the grading scale to be used (for example, 0-5) and set the criteria of the grading scales.
3. Students fill in the presenter's name on the blackline.
4. As students listen to the presentation, they fill in the points for each category.
5. At the end of the presentation, the presenter leaves the room.
6. Take the class average for each category.
7. Add the scores for the total and divide by five (for five categories).
8. The teacher will assign the final grade to each number.
9. The presenter is called back in and the scores are reviewed.

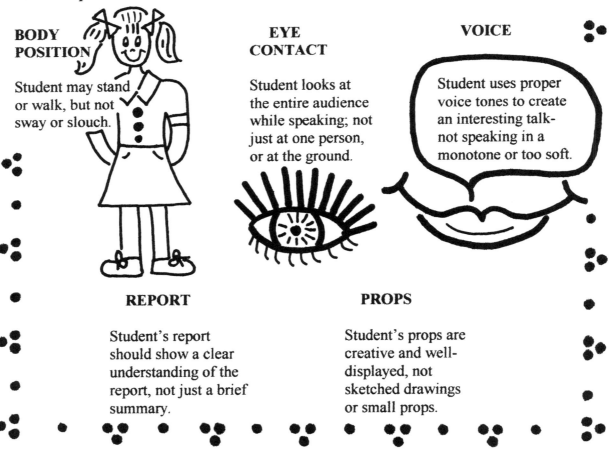

BODY POSITION
Student may stand or walk, but not sway or slouch.

EYE CONTACT
Student looks at the entire audience while speaking; not just at one person, or at the ground.

VOICE
Student uses proper voice tones to create an interesting talk- not speaking in a monotone or too soft.

REPORT
Student's report should show a clear understanding of the report, not just a brief summary.

PROPS
Student's props are creative and well-displayed, not sketched drawings or small props.

Presenter's Rubric

Name	Body Position	Eye Contact	Voice	Report	Props	Total

My _____ Rubric

Name_____Date_____

STATE OBJECTIVES ON EACH LINE

1._____

   0   1   2   3   4   5   6   7   8   9   10

2._____

   0   1   2   3   4   5   6   7   8   9   10

3._____

   0   1   2   3   4   5   6   7   8   9   10

4._____

   0   1   2   3   4   5   6   7   8   9   10

5._____

   0   1   2   3   4   5   6   7   8   9   10

6._____

   0   1   2   3   4   5   6   7   8   9   10

7._____

   0   1   2   3   4   5   6   7   8   9   10

8._____

   0   1   2   3   4   5   6   7   8   9   10

9._____

   0   1   2   3   4   5   6   7   8   9   10

10._____

   0   1   2   3   4   5   6   7   8   9   10

Step 11.Portfolio party plan

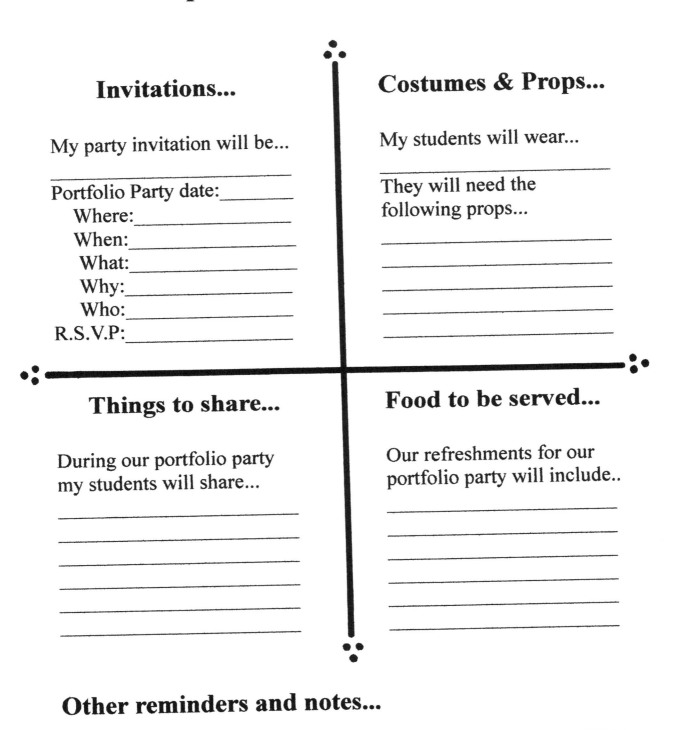

Invitations...

My party invitation will be...
_____
Portfolio Party date:_____
　　Where:_____
　　When:_____
　　What:_____
　　Why:_____
　　Who:_____
R.S.V.P:_____

Costumes & Props...

My students will wear...
_____
They will need the
following props...

_____
_____
_____
_____
_____

Things to share...

During our portfolio party
my students will share...

_____
_____
_____
_____
_____

Food to be served...

Our refreshments for our
portfolio party will include..

_____
_____
_____
_____

Other reminders and notes...

_____
_____

143

Step 12. Evaluate your unit

At the conclusion of your unit, make some notes of ways you can improve your unit next time. These suggestions and ideas could even make your unit better the next time you teach it. If you teach younger students, ask them the questions orally and you fill in their responses. You will be surprised at some of their ideas.

Teacher:
Things that worked best in my unit:

_____
_____
_____
_____

Things I should change the next time:

_____
_____
_____
_____
_____

Student:
My favorite part of this unit was:

_____
_____

Next time my teacher should:

_____
_____

Another subject I would like to study this year is:

_____

Chapter Eight

Find out what kind of homework the Bag Ladies have for you.

Homework

Find out what kind of homework the Bag Ladies have for you.

What would a bookbag be if it didn't contain homework? At our schools, the students use "agenda books" to learn the fine arts of organization and responsibility. If your school does not use these, there is a blackline included that we used to use with our students that accomplishes almost the same goals. Students copy their assignments daily and parents sign to say that they have seen the assignment given. By signing they are not saying that they have seen the finished product, in that we believe that this is the responsibility of the student. If the assignment is not completed, the teacher circles the assignment on the sheet or book, and writes, NOT DONE. In this way there is a daily communication with the parent and the student and the teacher.

Each Monday, we send out signed papers in a folder. These papers include both daily work and tests-everything except composition, which is kept in the student portfolio for portfolio theme parties. Parents are asked to look at the papers, sign the front of the folder, write optional comments (which we also do), and send back the folder with all papers. Included on the cover of the folder is a place where we mark the student's behavior on a scale of 1-4 and their homework responsibility on the same scale. I attach the front of the folders with rubber cement and can remove these fronts every semester to file for documentation of comments from the teacher and parent. All teachers usually have their own method of achieving this documenting, but this has always worked for us, and really comes in handy when needed!

Are you ready for your next assignment? Don't worry, this one is "in the bag" and very easy! If you like what you've read and are looking for a partner to plan with, or know someone else that might like these ideas, turn to the next page and follow the directions there. And THANKS for taking your assignments so seriously!

SIGNED PAPER FORM

			4 EXCELLENT
			3 GOOD
			2 FAIR
			1 WE NEED TO TALK

NAME _____ Quarter_____

DATE	PARENT'S SIGNATURE	COMMENTS AS NEEDED	BEHAVIOR HOMEWORK
			1 2 3 4 1 2 3 4
			1 2 3 4 1 2 3 4
			1 2 3 4 1 2 3 4
			1 2 3 4 1 2 3 4
			1 2 3 4 1 2 3 4
			1 2 3 4 1 2 3 4
			1 2 3 4 1 2 3 4
			1 2 3 4 1 2 3 4
			1 2 3 4 1 2 3 4

149

Student Weekly Assignment Sheet

Name_____Week of_____

SUBJECT	MON.	TUES.	WED.	THURS.	FRI.
SPELLING					
LANGUAGE					
WRITING					
MATH					
READING					
SOCIAL STUDIES					
SCIENCE & HEALTH					
CONDUCT					

150

Assignment Sheet Comments

Assignments are written on the chalkboard each day. Students are to copy them on the assignment sheet. Any assignments not completed at school become homework. All papers whether completed at school or to be finished at home should be in the student's work folder at the end of the day so parents can be sure the assignments are completed on time.

Parents, feel free to write comments at any time.

_____

_____

_____

_____

_____

_____

_____

PARENT'S SIGNATURE

Monday_____

Tuesday_____

Wednesday_____

Thursday_____

Friday_____

Magazine Cover Envelope

Materials needed...
*Old magazine covers, catalog covers, or heavyweight junk mail
*scissors   *Blank address label stickers   *One sheet
*Glue stick   *Writing pens or markers   of tagboard

*Use the envelope pattern to create your envelopes.

*Make a copy on tagboard and cut out.

*These envelopes work best if made from magazine covers
or heavier weight paper.

*Find a colorful magazine cover and trace the envelope
pattern on to the page.

*Cut out the envelope and fold as shown on the pattern at
the dotted lines.

*Glue the flaps down and insert your letter.

*On very colorful envelopes it works best to use blank address
label stickers to write addresses.

* Your envelope is ready to mail.

Dear _____,

How did you like the jazzy envelope that came in the mail for you today? It is just a sample of some exciting news I have for you! I just read the best book for teachers by the Bag Ladies! They are teachers just like us with the same crazy experiences at school and at home that we laugh about every day! The activities they demonstrate in their book really work for my students and the directions, illustrations, and photos make it visually clear! Even I can do it! They are helping me to write my own thematic unit with activities geared to my students! I'm looking for a partner to share ideas with. Could that be you?

Order the book *A Bookbag of The Bag Ladies' Best*, by contacting: Maupin House Publishing, 32 S.W. 42 Street, P.O. Box 90148, Gainesville, FL 32607, 1-800-524-0634 www.maupinhouse.com

Can you believe that these two teachers.... Oh, sorry, I don't want to ruin the book for you. Let me know when you're ready to start your unit!

Your friend in teaching,

_____

P.S. The directions for making the envelope are in the book, too!

CREATE AN ENVELOPE AS DIRECTED AND PUT A COPY OF THIS LETTER INSIDE. MAIL IT TO A TEACHER FRIEND AND IN NO TIME YOU WILL BE CREATING BAG LADY-STYLE UNITS!

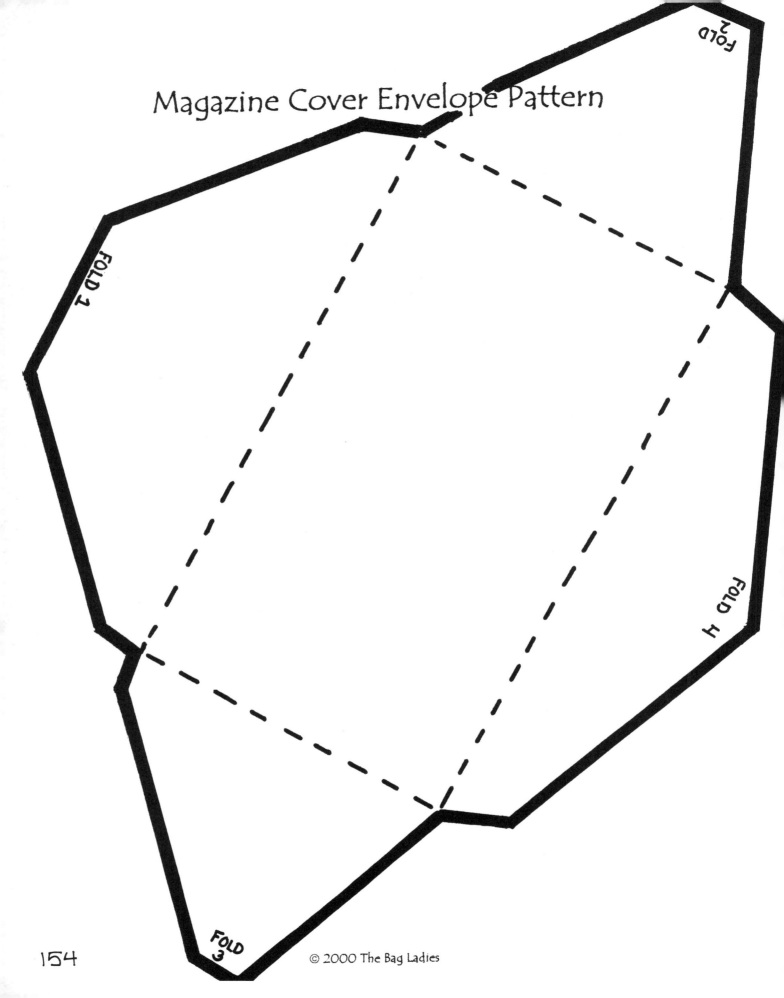

Magazine Cover Envelope Pattern

FOLD 2

FOLD 1

FOLD 4

FOLD 3

154

© 2000 The Bag Ladies

Chapter Nine

Become an honorary Bag Lady:
Here's how.

Graduation

Become an honorary Bag Lady: Here's how.

So, now it's easy to see that the Bag Ladies are teachers just like you. We both have spouses that want us to DO things on the weekends with them! We both have houses that are screaming for a dust rag and a mop! We have sporting events, homework projects, pets, dinners, and vacations to plan. We have birthday parties, presents, holidays, and classes to attend. All that and teaching, too! But, we found an easy way to do it all and enjoy our job. We hope that by reaching this chapter you, too, are saying, "I've become organized, I'm looking ahead, planning ahead, and creating a hands on classroom for my students and myself." We hope that you feel confident in writing a thematic unit of your own filled with exciting projects, where students actually apply the skills you have taught them. We sincerely hope that you have filled your students with the love of literature and how it motivates learning in all areas of the curriculum, even math! Mostly, we hope you have enjoyed rethinking about the goals of being a teacher that you had when you made the decision to follow this career. If you are saying, "Yes, yes, and even, maybe," then you have graduated from this "bookbag of ideas." We commend you and hope you enjoy your certificate. You earn it every day that you work with students!

Now for our present to you for reaching your goals. Just a few more Bag Lady tips and we'll be off, planning brand-new activities for you and your students, and, oh yes, still doing all the other "fun" chores of life and living.

Final tips for the graduate

(1) Keep your units in a notebook with page protectors. Label the notebook and keep it in the rubber container where you keep your thematic book, models of projects, and literature. When you are ready to teach the same theme the next year or even two years later, everything is together.

(2) Keep adding to the themes that you write. When on vacation or at a conference, browsing through a bookstore, you may find a book that goes well with a unit you have already completed. Throw it into the container and add it later.

(3) Make a model of all projects that you want to show students in your theme (don't worry, theirs will be much better). Then, at the end of the unit, keep your model and ONE of their models that you think is really good. Usually a student is flattered that you want to keep his or hers, just don't ask the same student every time.

(4) We used to collect factual materials to teach the unit. Now, we mainly use the district books, written materials, etc., given to us and just ADD to this.

(5) Most of all (and here is the biggest part of having a successful theme in your classroom), be excited, enthusiastic, challenging, and energetic in presenting what you are looking for, your objectives for the students, and the final product description. Your class will want to be as excited and motivated as you are!

We would love to hear from you. Please let us know if you are one of our honorary Bag Ladies and HAVE FUN!

OFFICIAL CERTIFICATE OF MERIT

Awarded to

_____

In Recognition for completing
your first Bag Lady-style unit
You are now an Honorary Bag Lady

Presented on _____
by Karen Simmons and Cindy Guinn

160

Some final "pointers" from the Bag Ladies

In all of our workshops we tell the participants that we like to think that we gave them some "pointers" during the day's presentation. Because of our primary classroom backgrounds, using actual pointers with students became as commonplace as using wordwalls and chart paper. Therefore combining the play on pointers and the actual pointer became a trademark of the Bag Ladies' Workshops. The more brainstorming we did about our theme activities, the more ideas for pointers followed.

For example, when we wrote "How Does Your Garden Grow," the pointer became the flower with the plastic 2-liter bottle butterfly attached to it. The students loved "flying" the butterfly from word to word. During the writing of "Ants, Bats, and Other Creatures," we agreed that the fly-swatter/word whacker was a great make-n-take for our students to whack their vocabulary words with.

Also, in the primary grades, students loved to take the pointer to the floor with the class "big-book" of the week and use it to point to the words as he/she read. Students amazingly learned more quickly at the language charts when using the pointers to point to the word that should be capitalized or where the punctuation mark should be placed. Gimmicks? Yes! Results? Definitely!

After we had both been "invited" to teach fourth grade we thought our "whacking" days were over. Have you looked at the vocabulary for the fifth grade math tests recently or the transition words for expository and/or narrative writing? There's a whole lot of "pointing and whacking" going on in the intermediate grades these days. We have found that the students love to learn words this way in all grade levels and even enjoy creating their own pointers to correspond with a story they have written or vocabulary they are trying to master.

Please enjoy looking over the pointers we have used in the past. Now, since you have just written your own thematic unit, what better time than the present to plan your pointer.

Finally, may we "point" out that sometimes the dowel rods are used for the "fun" of the portfolio party as in the theme "A Mathsquerade for the Millennium and Beyond," in which they attach a creative mask and all can enjoy the Mardi Gras atmosphere of the theme or as in "A Walk Across Florida," where a fish, dangling from the end of the dowel rod, holds a smaller fish, holding a calculator-paper story inside, to be shared with the portfolio guest at the end of the party.

Whatever your reason for your design, we hope we "pointed" you in the right direction (all right, enough on the play on words) in order to help you add this finishing touch to your unit!

Some final pointers from the Bag Ladies

Flower and Butterfly Pointer

Materials needed...
* 3/8 in. wooden dowel rod
* Clear plastic liter bottle
* Silk flower with stem
* One pipe cleaner
* Six in. length of thin gauge wire

Instructions...
(1) Twist the stem of the flower around the end of the dowel.
(2) Using the plastic under the label of a liter bottle, cut a pair of butterfly wings. Wrap the pipe cleaner around the center for a body.
(3) Use the wire to attach the butterfly to the flower.

Word Wacker Pointer
Materials needed...
* 6 in. X 4 in. piece of colored plastic canvas
* Two self-locking cable ties
* 3/8 in. wooden dowel rod

Instructions...
(1) Cut plastic canvas as pictured including a 1 in. wide, 3 in. long window in the center.
(2) To attach to dowel rod, string the cable ties through center and lock around dowel.

Multi-cultural Children Pointer

Materials needed...
*3/8 in. wooden
dowel rod
*Two multicultural
children cutouts
*Scotch tape
*Yarn scraps
*Fabric scraps
*Markers

Instructions...
(1) Decorate each of
your multi-cultural
cutouts using markers,
yarn, and fabric.
(2) To attach to dowel,
lay one of the cutouts
right side down on the
table. Tape back side to
the end of the dowel.
(3) To attach the second
shape, glue to cover tape.

Mask Pointer

Materials needed...
*3/8 in. wooden
dowel rod
*Cheap white
paper plate
*Curling ribbon
(assorted colors)
*Glitter glue
*Feathers
*Other small
decorations
*Scissors

Instructions...
(1) Cut a mask shape from
the paper plate including
holes for eyes.
(2) Cut two small slits in
one side of paper plate to
attach mask to dowel.
Tie in place with curling
ribbon and leave hanging.
(3) Decorate mask with
glitter glue, feathers, and
other decorations.

Beaded Bug Bubble Pointer

Materials needed...
* 1 yd. 26-gauge wire
* 3/8 in. wooden dowel rod
* Assorted sizes of acrylic or glass beads

Instructions...
(1) Fold the wire in half and twist up from fold approximately 2 inches.
(2) String one bead through one wire, then second bead through both wires. Continue for about 2 inches.
(3) Split the wires and create two loops that meet in the middle (forming wings).
(4) Hold the wires together and thread three to five more beads.
(5) Separate the wires again to form antennae, trim, and curl.
(6) Attach bug to dowel rod by twisting wire at the bottom of the bug and cover with tape.

*This pointer can be used as a bubble wand.

Fishing Rod Pointer

Materials needed...
* 3/8 in. wooden dowel rod
* Two colors of craft foam
* One self-locking cable tie
* 2 1/2 ft. of heavy yarn

Instructions...
(1) Cut two circles 3-4 in. in diameter. Cut one handle as shown in the picture.
(2) To attach circles and handle, string cable tie through each piece so dowel is in the middle.
(3) Tie yarn from reel to rod.

Chapter Ten

We don't want to leave you "Up in the Air," so here
are some lifelines in the form of blacklines.
Copy masters to make your life easier.

Pop-Up Book

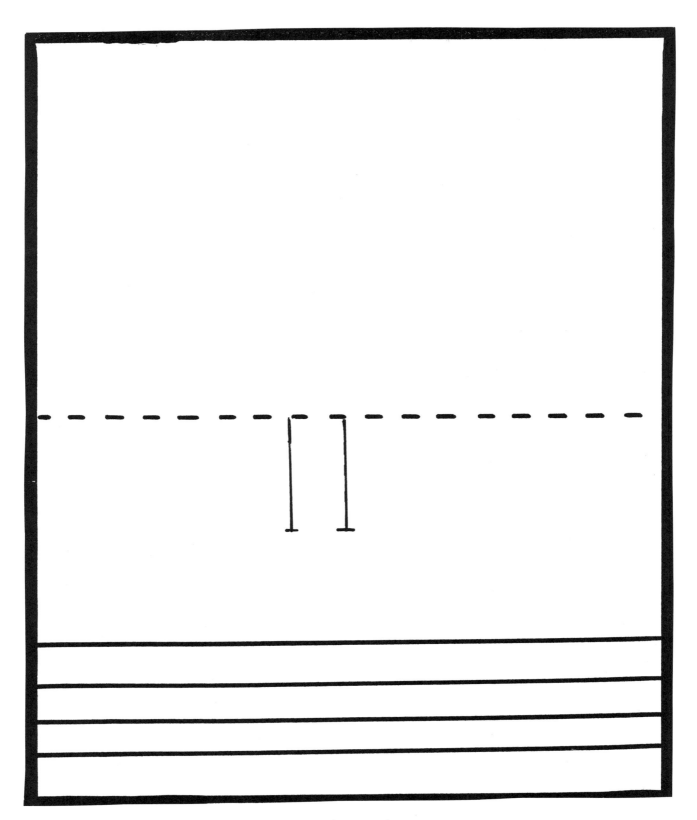

Pop-Out Book

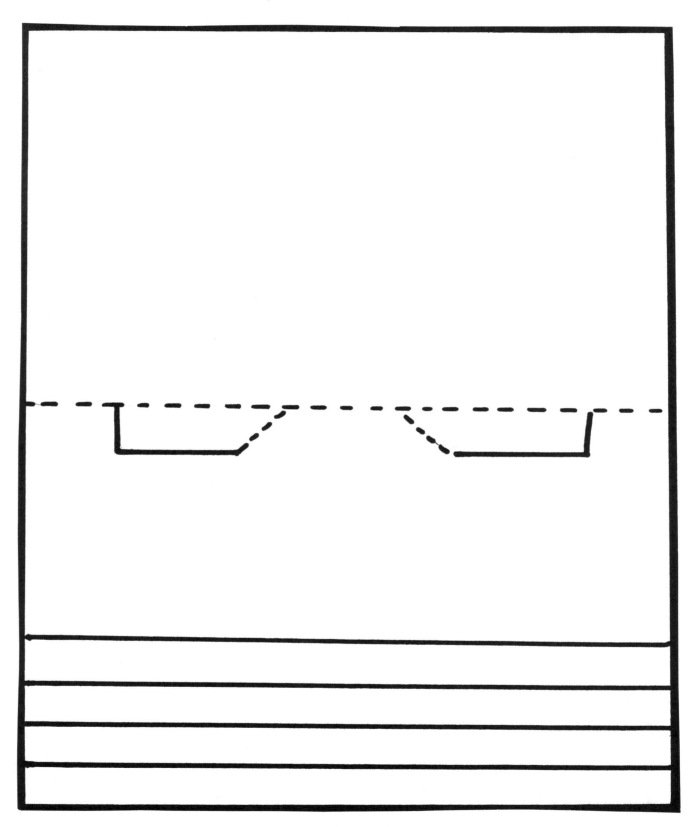

Characters Through the Page

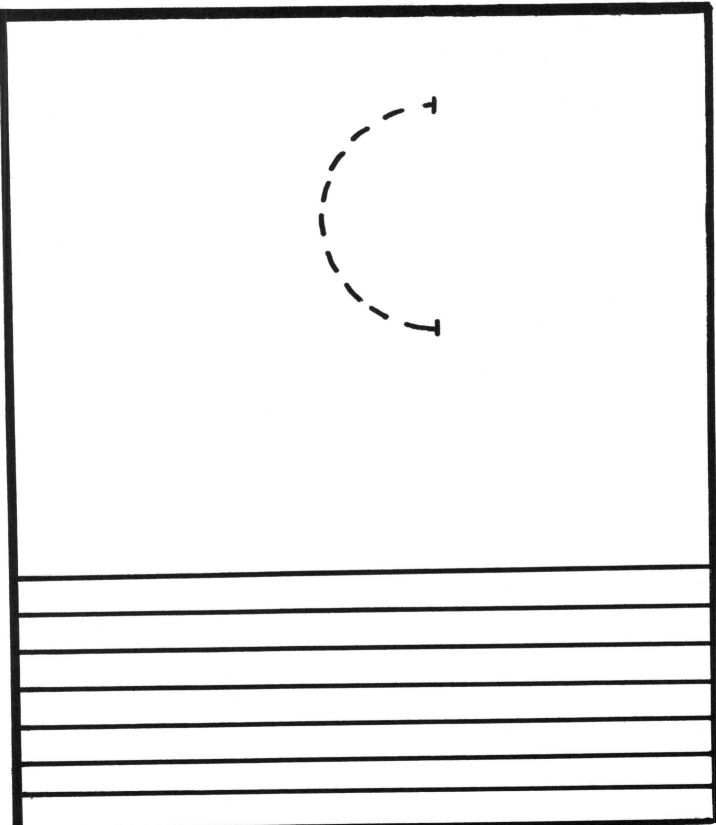

See-Through Book

Character Flipbook

Magnet Activities

Flip-Flop-Fold Book

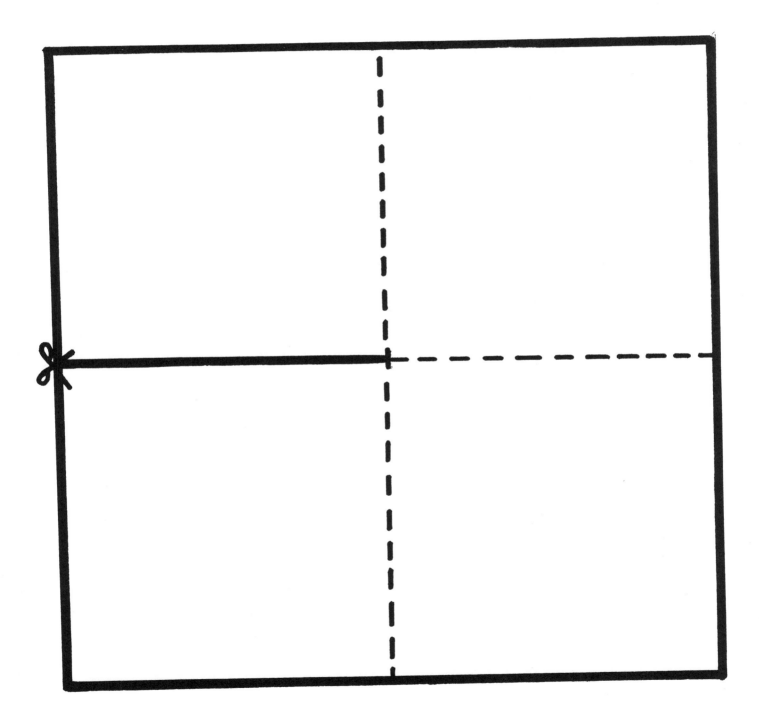

175

Character Slide-Through Book

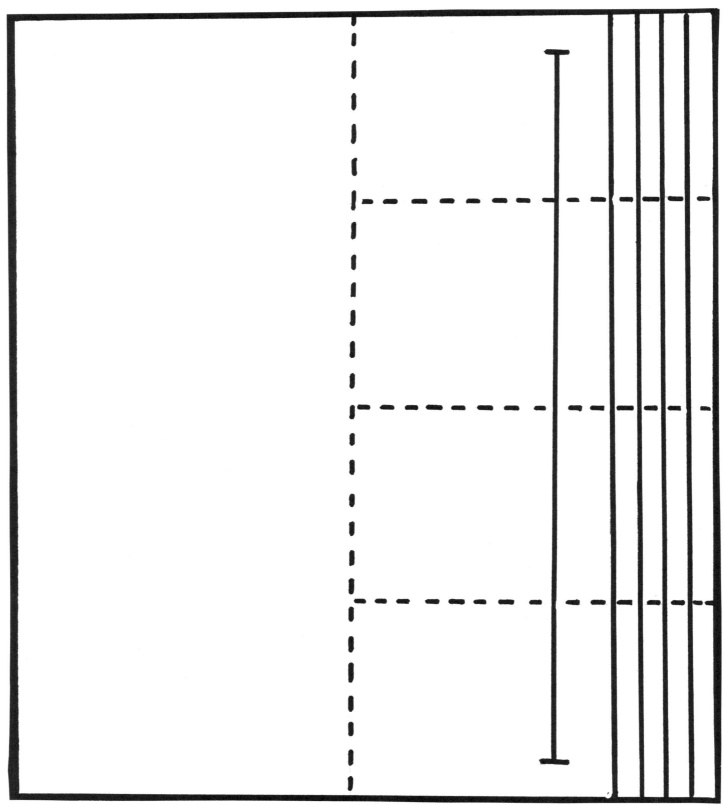

A-B-C Big Book

is for _____

No-Glue Book – page 1

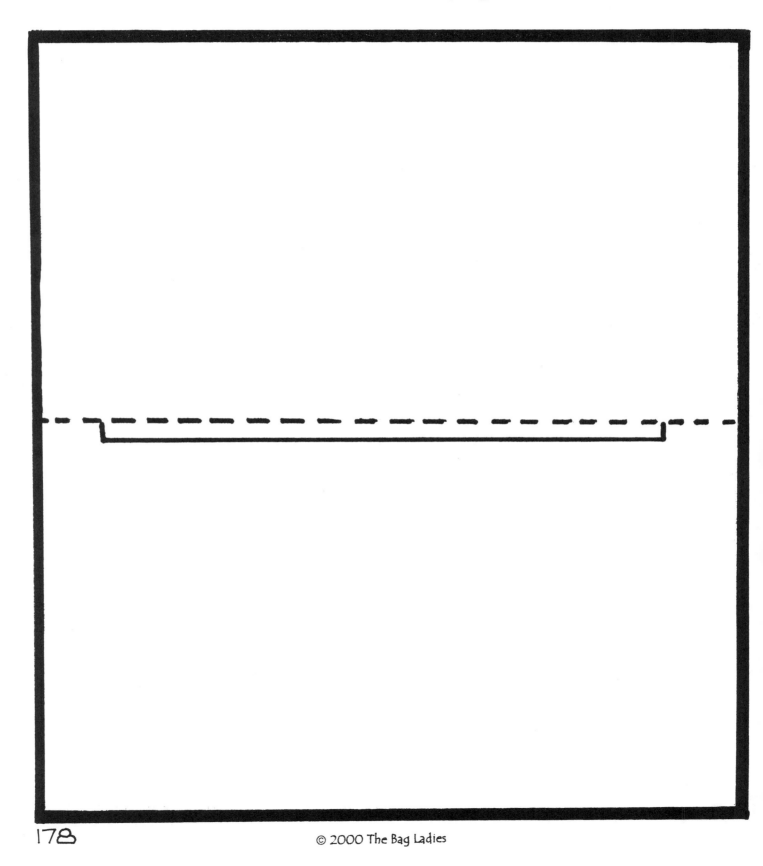

No-Glue Book - page 2

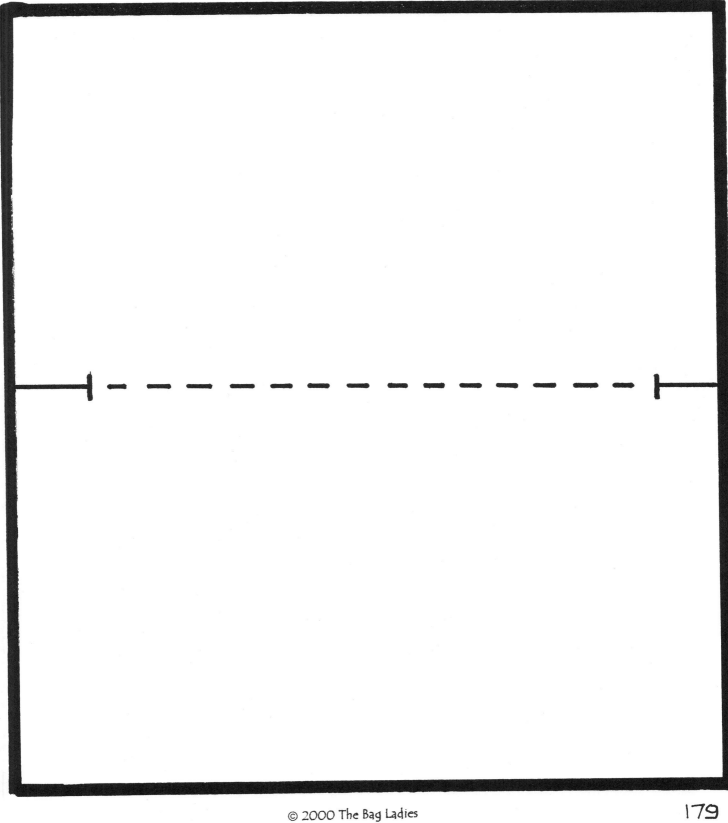

179

Step Book -page 1

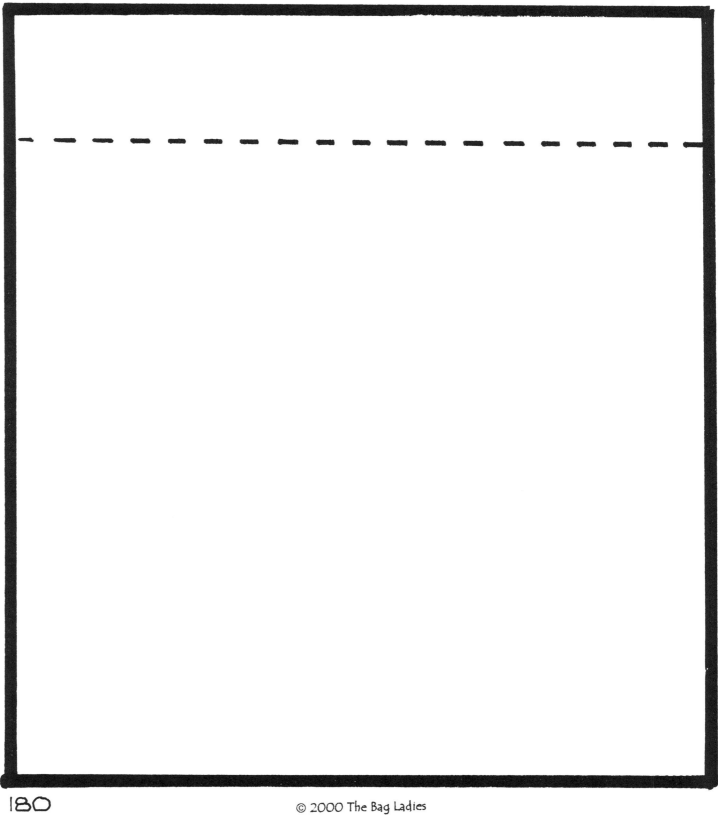

Step Book - page 2

Seed Packet Book - page 1

183

Seed Packet - page 2

_____

MY TOPIC

(DESCRIBE) _____

_____

_____

_____

_____

INTERESTING FACT #1: _____

_____

_____

INTERESTING FACT #2: _____

_____

_____

SPECIAL FEATURES: _____

_____

_____

_____

VOCABULARY & DEFINITIONS: _____

_____

_____

_____

Postcard Book

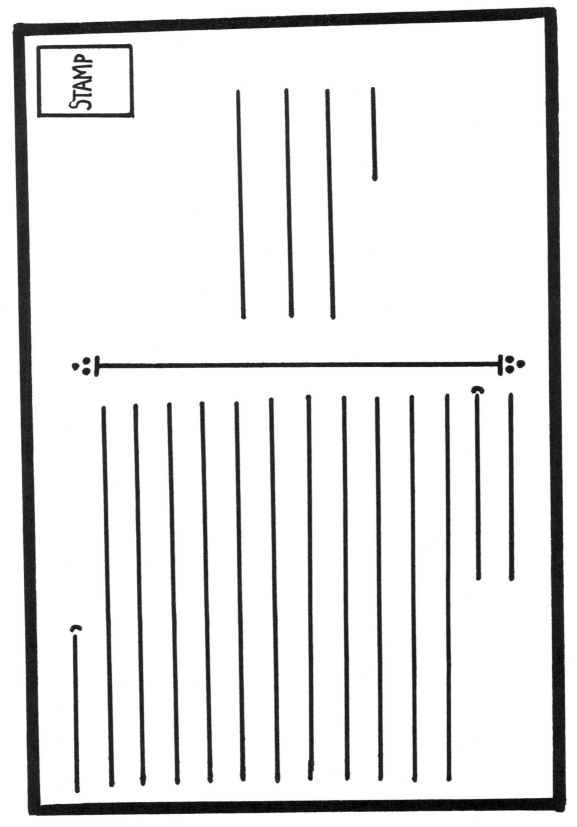

STAMP

185

Filmstrip Project

186

Bag Lady-Style Brochure – page 1

OTHER INFORMATION...

THE AUTHOR...

Bag Lady-Style Brochure - page 2

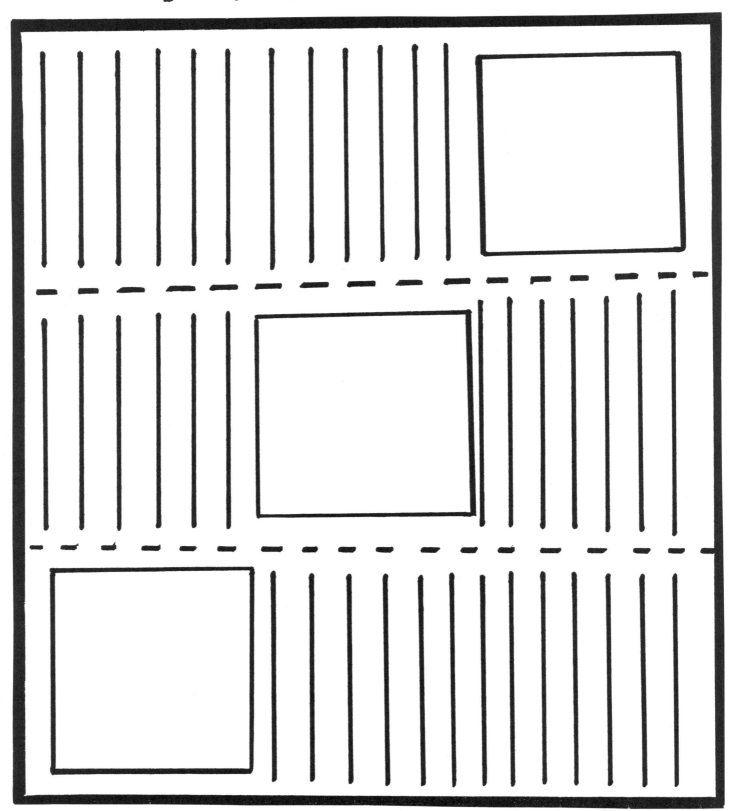

Daily Times News

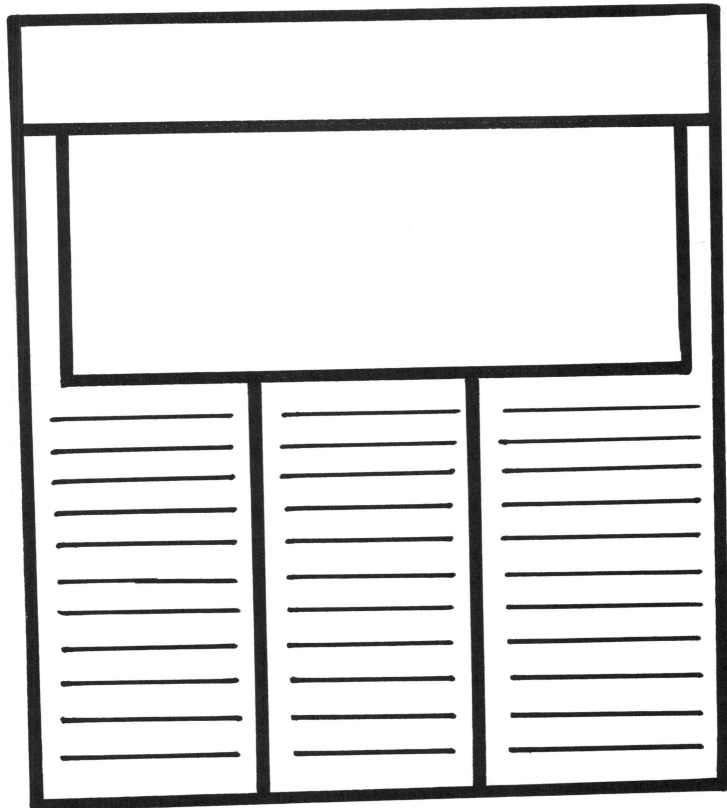

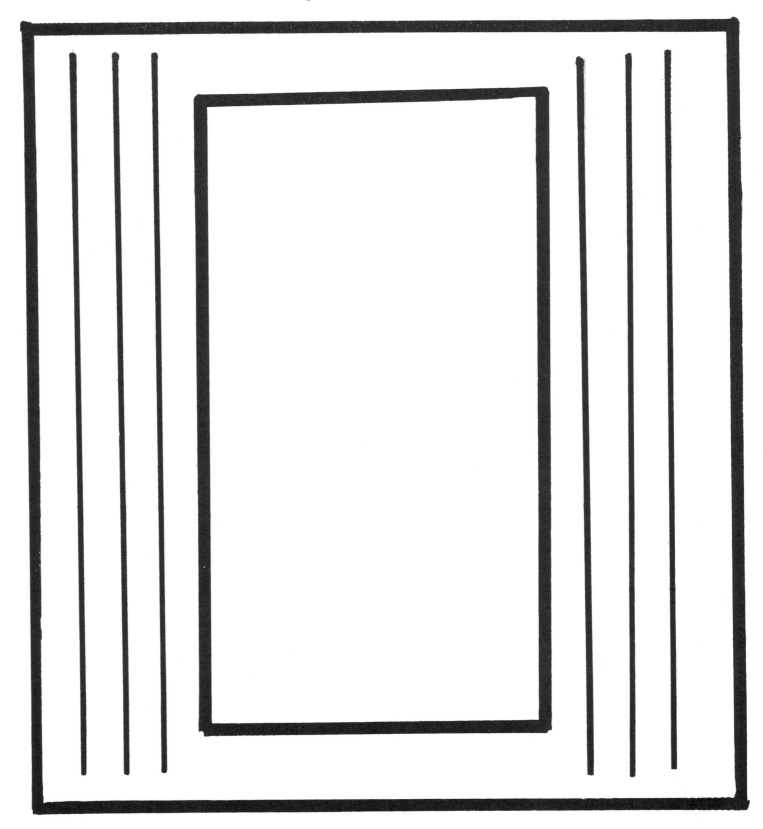

Overlay Book - page 2

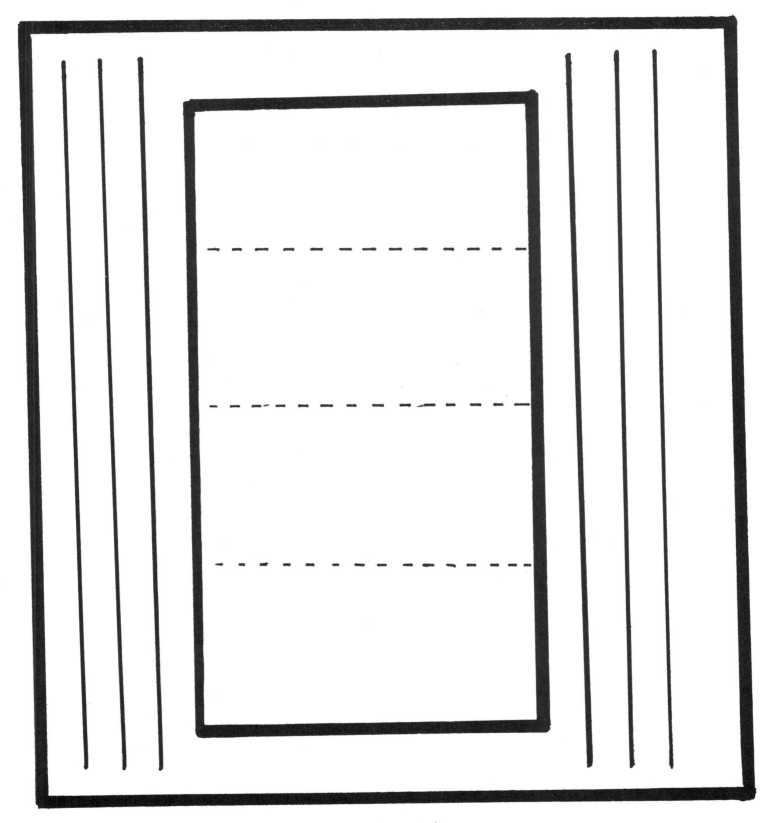

191

Cereal Box Projects

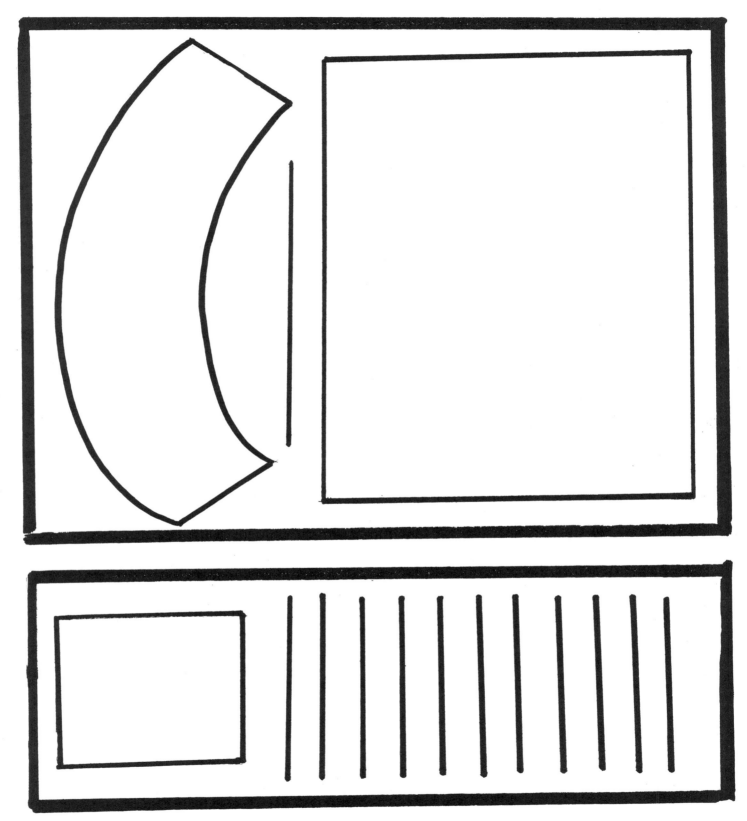

Cereal Box Projects

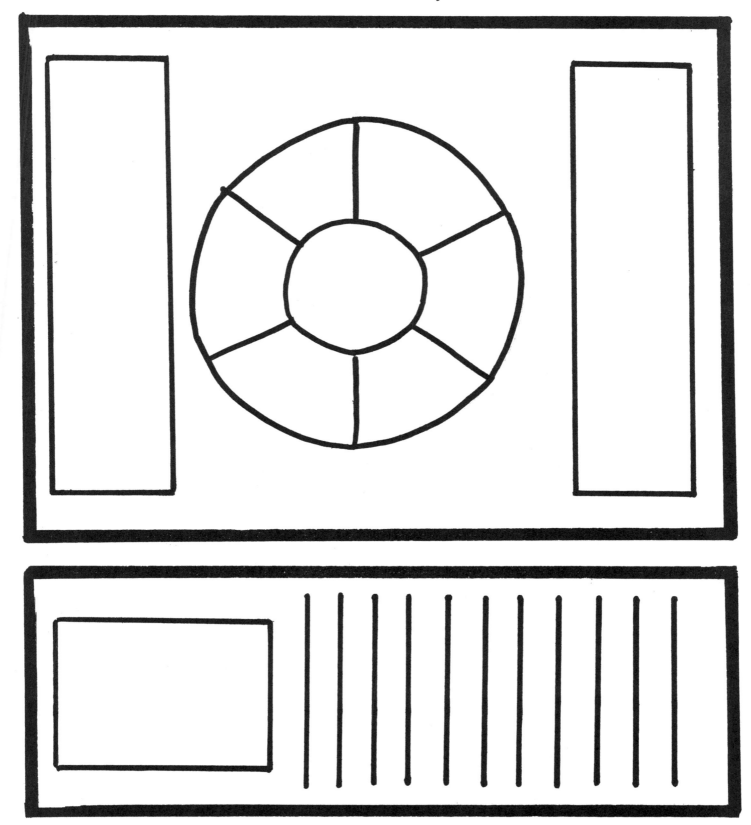

193

Index

Order Form

Quantity	Title	Price	Tax	Total
_____	How Does Your Garden Grow	17.00	1.02	_____
_____	Up in the Air	17.00	1.02	_____
_____	Lights, Cameras, Shadows, Actions	17.00	1.02	_____
_____	Ants, Bats, and Other Creatures	17.00	1.02	_____
_____	Kids, Colors, Quilts	17.00	1.02	_____
_____	Hats Off to the USA	17.00	1.02	_____
_____	Our Classroom Becomes an Ancient Egyptian Museum	17.00	1.02	_____
_____	Recycling After the Picnic	17.00	1.02	_____
_____	A Walk Across Florida	17.00	1.02	_____
_____	Book Talks	17.00	1.02	_____
_____	Writing Thoughts	17.00	1.02	_____
_____	A Mathsquerade for the Millennium and Beyond	17.00	1.02	_____
_____ new	Readin', Writin', and Rithmetic'	17.00	1.02	_____
_____ new	The Poetry Pouch	17.00	1.02	_____
		SUBTOTAL		_____
		Shipping and handling 10%		_____
		TOTAL		_____

Mail order to: Bag Ladies
PMB 256
1128 Royal Palm Beach Blvd.
Royal Palm Beach, FL 33411

(561) 793-8268 (561) 793-3955
Bagladiesonline.com

Ship to: Name_____
Address_____
_____
City_____
State/zip_____
Phone_____
Email_____